thanks and SORRY and good luck

REJECTION
LETTERS
FROM THE
EYESHOT
OUTBOX

LEE KLEIN

BARRELHOUSE BOOKS

BALTIMORE, MARYLAND, USA

BARRELHOUSE BOOKS

For information about permission to reproduce selections from this book, please write to:

Barrelhouse Books
PO Box 17598
Baltimore, MD 21297-1598

Visit our website at www.barrelhousemag.com

ISBN 978-0-9889945-2-2
Library of Congress Control Number: 2014931584

EDITOR
Mike Ingram

BOOK DESIGN AND LAYOUT
Anastasia Miller

"Illusion is the first of all pleasures."

Oscar Wilde

FOREWORD

by Matthew Simmons

For a while there all we wanted to do was publish our stories on the internet. And so we surfed around and around—our stories saved onto our hard-drives, waiting—and we looked and we looked for a place to publish them. We read stories on the internet, and we read the bios of the story writers, and we saw all the places that were publishing their work. And if their stories were in any way like our stories, we sent them to the places that had published them. We sat and waited. We checked our email regularly. We checked our email for responses from the websites. Responses arrived. And, for the most part, we got rejections. Most of them were generic. Thanks, but no thanks. Move it along. Try again, or don't. Whatever.

The best thing about writing fiction for publication on the internet was getting a rejection letter from Lee Klein at Eyeshot.

The best. Seriously. Lee was funny. Lee was direct. Lee was fucking merciless. Lee was exactly what we all needed when we were working to get better at whatever it was we were trying to get better at. He was there, holding our feet to the fire. He was there, responding intelligently and thoughtfully. And really damn quickly. And he was, it seemed, really enjoying himself.

His rejections sometimes felt like a prolonged, broken narrative, a story being sent out to the world, one person at a time. Luckily for us, he saved them.

Here's a thing to try: Become an editor for an online journal. Start responding to submissions. Read tons and tons of work. See how long it takes before you start rejecting stories with: "Can't use this at this time. Good luck finding a home for it elsewhere."

It takes a couple of months. (It took me a couple of months, at least.)

REJECTION LETTERS FROM THE EYESHOT OUTBOX

But you never got a rejection like this from Lee. He had an astonishing amount of editorial energy. You took the work you sent him seriously. He responded in kind. Even when his rejections were at their most playful, you always had the sense that what you wrote was given a shot. A thorough going-through. Eyeshot has been around for more than a decade, and for many of those years Lee was doing exactly this: honestly reacting to the work writers were sending him. And it's honesty that every writer needs, even if it's not always what every writer wants.

Lee Klein is the father of internet literature. I'm just going to go out on a limb and say that. He owns us all. So thanks, internet-writing Dad. I wouldn't be where I am today without you.

"A recent message we received doubted whether we ever actually reject submissions. We provide this compilation to prove that indeed we do not accept everything sent to the site. If you notice that one of the letters below was originally sent to you, that's good, it means you have swallowed your pride and returned. If not, if you have never seen one of these letters, please submit — maybe you too will receive your very own personalized rejection."

Note preceding the first batch of rejection letters
posted to Eyeshot.net on November 16, 2001

Thank you for sending this submission for our consideration. Due to the number of submissions we receive a day, we are unable to comment on the work. Please realize that we appreciate (and even respect) your impulse to transmit material for potential posting on our online literary internet e-webzine, yet we are faced with the simple problem of too many submitters, not enough time to respond in detail to them all. If this response were seen from close up, it would include myriad analyses, concise suggestions, and conciliatory curlicues. Thanks to the number of submissions we receive, however, we are only able to provide a macroresponse, one visible from somewhere very high above, and, up in the netherworlds where no winged creature born of bird can propel and sustain itself, our response, nearly embedded in earth far below, simply looks like two vertical/parallel lines of equal height connected by a swift diagonal from the head of the western line to the foot of the eastern one (i.e., "N"), accompanied a few clicks eastward by a complementary-sized circle (i.e., "O"). Thank you. And good day.

Eyeshot's Failed Attempt at a Form Rejection Letter

Thank you for thinking your submission would look good on Eyeshot. I wish it would, too! I could tell you what would make it better, for us, from our perspective. I could tell you, but I won't. You teach writing already, you should know. Be a good teacher. I will tell you, just a little, employing the magic of metonymy. When referring to the chocolate-covered candy, "M&M" is the preferred spelling. Also, here's why in your own words: "we're not happy with things not being of a certain profoundness." And our new motto? "Confound the new French feminists!" Fall in love "with our discourse, with our theoretical perspectives, whatever makes the attraction work," then go write new stuff. This will "not be the only opportunity you will ever have." You are well wished.

Eyeshot's In Favor of Changing the Word for
"Setting Sun" to Something Simpler, like "20"

The word "rusted" at the end of the first paragraph. The modifier-hanging-after-comma thing you did with the word "abandoned" to end the second paragraph. There should be a law. I suggest you be careful with that in the future, vigilant. Don't go hanging those things: they're like curveballs. If you hang one, it better cut quick, fall off the table, otherwise, punk-ass editors like me gonna knock that junk out. But such things can be snipped. And I would suggest snipping if I liked the overall story. But it's like a roving webcam that doesn't do anything but show what's known — it also seems to think its pixilated distortion is all pretty and shit. It's a short piece that's stylized in a way I don't get off on. Sorry for the attack. I get that way sometimes. I do it because I used to get form-letter rejections all the time, and I started the site in part to treat submitting writers as I'd like to be treated. A little rough sometimes, always honest, letting everyone know exactly why. The rejection has nothing to do with you or your children or your way of life. Only the piece of writing you sent me. You and it are different. I wrote about what you wrote. Anyway, if you're not too blustered by this note, and you ever feel like submitting anything again, please do.

Eyeshot's Evil Empire

I read through all FIVE submissions and don't think any of them are really right for the site. I usually give the 718 a little leeway, but sorry, these are pretty rough and not so funny, though obviously intended to be funny — and you should never submit more than one piece at a time — it pisses editors off, since most submitters submit only one at a time, then submit another upon rejection, that's the way it's done... but I don't really care about that — I had the time just now to look through them, and what you sent falls flat for me — but hey it falls flat for ME only — I'm hard to please sometimes, especially when it comes to humor, although my only requirement is that, at least once, I laugh out loud. So maybe try these somewhere else, or try to write something a little more ambitious, or try to write something that doesn't so obviously TRY to be funny... My guess is you're pretty young? Spending spring break submitting to weird lit sites or something? Anyway, thanks for submitting and try me again if you want, but next time, send one piece at a time.

At first I thought you took some pages from a Frank McCourt memoir, copied them, then added a dash of Pac-Man. I liked a lot of this, the parts that seemed most authentic about life in Dublin, staring into the fire and the conflict between helping others or not (as well as the potential depression related to not helping). But then there were little whimsical flashes, like you didn't want this to be all that serious, though it seemed like it wanted to be more serious than it was. It had a certain gravity pulling it nicely toward seriousness, but something in you kept popping up and winking about lesbian intrigue or Pac-Man, undercutting the established tone. I like that it's more substantial and not as impatient in terms of super-quick movement, but this still doesn't quite feel right for this site. I liked a lot of it and at times wavered toward being more positive but the ending nudged me toward writing this little explanatory note. Thanks again and sorry and good luck elsewhere!

I'm not really sure this is a story — I mean, you could call it one, if you wanted to. But still. It's like a really short short-short. And it seems more like editorial than art, I think. I could see it mixed in with other super-short testaments from "today's work force" in a magazine or newspaper. The so-called "literary short short" I think maybe might require more poetics, maybe might need to seem more like a prose poem, denser, with more associative meaning? Not that it "needs" but that that sort of thing seems more "successful" when it's more "poetic"? I really like the thing about college kids aggressively breaking down boxes — that could be a good story — but you'd have to wrangle it all, right? When I've written about shitty jobs I've worked, I think I've realized that close reportage of the actual doesn't really do it for the reader — you might satisfy yourself, but you have to think about a reader's expectations, as you would an amorous compatriot in bed. As it is, what you sent seems more like half-conscious autoerotic strokes of a semi-erect member, maybe while watching TV — by which I mean the autoerotic or self-serving element isn't all that exciting for the viewer, not even from a voyeuristic perspective. Anyway, it looks like this rejection has doubled your submission's word count. Good luck and definitely send something a little more developed some day.

Eyeshot's Voyeuristic Vacuum

Sorry it took me so long to reply. I guess I got the message right around Christmas and was home and otherwise engaged for a few days, you know that period between Xmas and New Year's Day when it's always too bright out because you're always a bit hungover and indoors too often, but now I'm back and ready to initiate the Year in Rock that will one day be known as 2001, reading manuscripts, and let me tell you, I voted for Gore, but that was only because I didn't want Bush in office and Nader seemed like a lefty Perot, in terms of his ultimate effect on the election. So, what does this mean to you? Not sure. It means I liked your story enough and would accept it under some circumstances, but right now, what with the new year and all, we want to start out banging and overthrow the illegitimate Bush regime with weird online lit, and the story you submitted is a lot like its narrator, it's a smooth read that doesn't jump out of its skin too much? If I were married to it, I'd cheat too. Susan Sontag once wrote about husband and lover-type writers, and I think the same can be applied to stories. It's a husband story, but we're looking for something a little more wild and unprotected and wet. Something erotic, if not ever involving anything sexy. Sontag called for an erotics of hermeneutics. Eyeshot calls for an erotics of online lit.

Thank you for submitting again, but we're gonna pass on this — and not even tell you why at any length. I just quit smoking — and the story ends with talk of quitting smoking, and so, perhaps because I need a damn cigarette, I couldn't get into the story's conclusion so well. Sorry — my fault, not yours — oh well, a little your fault, too. But if I were more awake, a better/less distracted reader, and if I were huffing on a cigarette, maybe you'd have a better chance, but alas, you know how things work: right place, right time. It's really a shame that smoking has detrimental health effects. It's a shame that holding a little bit of fire so close to one's face makes it hard to get in a semblance of shape. Harder to run around the dustbowl track in McCarren Park when lungs still seem filled with the exhalations of everyone out last night at Enid's. But we will round into shape. We will run and not smoke and become strong again. We hope the same for you and your writing. Your writing consists of lungs and legs. May they be clean and strong. Thanks again for submitting.

Thank you for submitting. I can't use it for Eyeshot. I'm having one of those days in which I can't explain myself. You ever have one of those days? You make decisions but you can't come close to arranging words into sentences about these decisions, yet you're still confident you're making the right ones? Some days I'm all intuition... All I can say is sorry and please send more stuff one day.

Thanks for the nice words about the site. I think what you sent reads clearly and makes sense (more than some submissions) but I think it might read a little too clearly and make a little too much sense for Eyeshot. I like what you sent more or less, I guess, although it's difficult to gauge in terms of readerly enjoyment. You present a nostalgic pleasure principle best-case scenario alternative, and although I liked the bit about the Pirates and would love to post something about the late '70s team with Dave Parker and Stargell and how they meshed with the Steelers (L.C. Greenwood, Rocky Bleier), but I think for me to accept this for Eyeshot, it would have to veer and swerve a lot more, like instead of getting a job at the paper, he'd work on a farm but the farm would be no ordinary farm, it'd be directly responsible for the success of the 1978 Pirates season, and then due to a particularly dry winter, the next season, the Pirates would do terribly and you'd have to fight day and night to milk the cows and pour the milk into particular furrows that correspond to particular positions on the diamonds, like a voodoo farm in western Pennsylvania or something — it would start out straight but then get stranger and stranger, entertaining folks along the way with witticisms and observations and whatnot. So. That being said, I think I won't accept this but I will thank you for submitting and I hope you keep reading the site.

Eyeshot's Dale Berra

It's all intuition. And the "aura" of this one is sort of like a freckly yellow, which reminds me of bananas, which doesn't make me want to post it. That's a really terrible critique, I realize.

Thanks for thinking this might be right for Eyeshot. Unfortunately, we're really hesitant to touch anything involving Lucifer, the Prince of Darkness. We're hesitant for obvious reasons, mostly involving eternal damnation, not only in the afterlife but in this one as well, particularly in terms of literary values and shit like that. Now, I'm a fan of a good devil story if the devil is, say, one's parrot, or one's car key and it's trying to compel you to either make it repeat the word "horseshoe" or run it along your friend's already beaten-up, rundown, rust-worn Hyundai, got me? Ultimately, "Devil's Dung" is not something we're interested in right now, and probably never will be until it's a Ben & Jerry's flavor.

Eyeshot's Splattered Dog Dessert

Apologies for the delayed response. We're usually very quick. In a submission-response race with five other sites, we won by 21 days, responding in 16 seconds. Swear to G-d. Twenty seconds after you submitted I read the first bit, then got distracted. I came back to it again, then again, then again, then again, then again, and then finally with a fresh head, and alas, there's a reason I kept coming back to it: I couldn't really get into it. Sorry. It's sort of a travelogue trip thing, which is fine if it involves a relatively unknown country, unlike France. It's cool to write about restoring French castles, but only if you mention Aleister Crowley, who is English. Beware of "beckoning vineyards" and "walking forlornly." The submission's not really fiction, right? And so it seems like the time there was reward enough. Putting the piece up wouldn't be right. Sorry. I know you see more in what you've sent than I do, and that's very cool, since the lines are filled with other things you didn't or just couldn't mention. And even if you got all those things down in print, I'm not sure it would be right. Ultimately, I'd prefer for Eyeshot not to shelter stories about My Interesting Experience Abroad.

Eyeshot's Droopy Dragnet of Buttery French Chicks

Hi. Sorry it took so long to get back to you. I just had a look. I liked how it started. But then couldn't keep track of it. A few lines threw me off. Now, I'm neither daft nor an elaborate fuckwit, despite being an American, nor am I particularly hungover, and in general I like these kind of long, some would say overambitious, semi-impressionistic sentences. You can see them all over Eyeshot. I'm more interested in reading, writing, and posting stuff that focuses more sentence-to-sentence than on an organized, polished, well-plotted, dull-as-fuck whole. The thing, though, for the web particularly, I think there needs to be a little more energy and humor in the voice to maintain the line-to-line momentum. It's essentially a rambling story. And rambling stories need more than just breath to sustain to the end, especially over seven pages. Go England! Kill the Krauts!

Eyeshot's Flophouse for American Football Enthusiasts

                a l t
   h o
u g h

            u
   haven't
quite

      managed to spell
            "elaboratley
                  concieved"...
         c o r r e c t l y

w
 e
  d
    o
     t
     h
    a
   n
  k
  y
   o
    u
          f o r
      your
  c
    o
      n
       s
        i
   d
   e
    r
      a
       t
        i
     o
  n.

please note: back-to-back spelling errors are not sufficient grounds for denial: just my sugar levels were low, and i'd have to be out-of-mind wacked on a 12-pack of cola to really want to post what you sent. unfortunately i am not wacked on lots of cola; thus, will not post your submission. do not let this affect your day. if you live on the east coast of america it is beautiful today, if a little windy. a good day to lie around and ejaculate into a latex sack coated with spermicidal lubricant — tell me truthfully: did you labor nine months on the submitted poem? don't lie. are you really its mama then? not that you need to take nine months on a short poem for a pathetically undertrafficked literary-like website, but, but, but: thank you for liking what you saw on the site and submitting (to Allah). what we mean is: thank you for playing.

G A M E O V E R

PLEASE TRY AGAIN.

INSERT COIN(S)

9 8 7 6 5 4 3 2 1 0

Alcalde; El Barrio del Ojos Tirados
(mayor; the ghetto of thrown eyes)

REJECTION LETTERS FROM THE EYESHOT OUTBOX

Hi. It's a little too spare. Too cool. Sorry. But thanks. Please try again, maybe with something longer.

Hi — So... Raskov. As in *Crime and Punishment*. Um, ok. I'd be interested in this if it were more than an imitation — if you took Raskolnikov's personality (whose name means "split") and did some things and told some stories and made them entertaining and funny and odd in a way that undermined the idea of Raskolnikov... But all you really do is present a stripped-down letter and the reaction, with an eye-rolling conclusion about children being our future. The main thing I'd think about would be something like "who do you think would be reading this?" and "what would they like to read?" and "how does one go about making people happy?" I'm sorry if this message won't make you happy but you might want to think about what it is that people want to read and why and when you have an idea to write something like what you've written (a good idea), you might think a little bit about how you can work from that idea rather than just fulfilling it, how you can launch off of it and entertain people and surprise yourself too instead of just sort of filling the slot. Anyway — thanks for submitting again and sorry if that makes three rejections — this ain't baseball!

George "the Animal" Steele can put his fat-ass head in a blender and send me the salsa. I'm having a party this weekend and need something gelatinous to feed and fatten the marsupials before the slaughter. Puree of opossum imported from Papua, New Guinea, stuffed with a George "The Animal" Steele and white-bean cilantro garnish: scrumptious — *totalmente* deeeeeliciosa! What scatological pungency as pungently foul and as twist of tongue smells so much of long labor's sweat? *Y si tu quieres recibir el spam,* well, tu haf 2 input tu address electronica: you'll get it. You'll get it real soon, mister drowsy-chimpansy-swingin'-from-a-cock-n-ball trapeze. Three weeks is a long time. A long time to have your face held flush against the encrusted porcelain of eternity's watery vortex. By which I mean it's always a pleasure to receive your submissions, Herr Fliegen, but this one we shan't accept.

Eyeshot's Complex of Thin-Skinned Tears

Hi. You're pretty young, huh? 15? I wrote a pretty nasty message below, but now feel bad because you're almost half my age. I searched for your e-mail address on google and found out you're not what your note says you are, that is, not an adult NYC freelance writer but a precocious teen from New England. The thing you sent doesn't work. You can't write the way you wrote about the WTC thing, unless you really pull it off like *The Onion* did in late September with its HOLY FUCKING SHIT! headline. If you want me to go into it more, I will. Anyway, here's what I would have sent if you were actually an adult NYC freelance writer... In the future, we suggest you don't use the following words:

personal (to describe an essay)

besotted (to describe a day)

occasional

tragicomic (to describe a fucking disaster)

travails

solace

poignant

overwrought

denizens (especially not modified by overwrought)

We'll accept your friend's blessed trinity of rude, crude, removed — it's close to what we're after — but "Poor Man's McSweeney's"? Such statements in your intro are contraindicated, and Eyeshot's layout is based on Suck.com and Ubu.com. You brought blood to my brain. Meet me at 9 pm for a duel of chicken bones and hot sauce, somewhere near the L train — at the KFC at 14th and 3rd. I will show you rude and crude. I will teach you the meaning of removed. I will show you what happens when eager talent is misdirected. Anyway, thank you for submitting, and glad you like the site, but the piece does not meet our poor man's standards. Best wishes for finding a home for your "personal essay."

Eyeshot's Cracked Skull of Wheezing Fire
(P.S. Good luck!)

REJECTION LETTERS FROM THE EYESHOT OUTBOX

Excuse me for sounding like that senator debating Dan Quayle, but I know Joyce very well, and you are no James Joyce. I'm familiar with what J.J. does and how he does it. And I see what you're doing, somewhat. But I think the "experimental" parts of the text, the fragmentation, get in the way more than do much good. And the lines, the prose of it, is/are more like stream-of-Bukowski than anything "stylistic." What I mean is that there's a difficult-to-get-through thing (i.e., tension, muddledness) happening between the simplicity of the sentences and the overall style. Or more so, there's a sort of experimental/pretentious conceit to the way you present the episodes (i.e., jump cut) within the story (call it "the whole") that's not matched by an equivalent experimentation/pretension line by line (call it "the parts"). Got that? So that's why I think it's ok for me to apologize and say thank you for submitting, thanks for considering the piece good for Eyeshot etc, but in the end, I think it might benefit from some more work, or maybe from cutting it up into smaller pieces that then are worked on a little more... dunno. Anyway, thanks, and please send more when you have more. Points for degree of difficulty were awarded, just execution wasn't quite there.

Eyeshot's Exagmination Round Our Work in Progress

Thanks for submitting. It's always nice to get submissions. Nice to have something to read that someone wants you to read (if you're reading this message aloud please make it sound like "wants" in the previous sentence is italicized: thanks). Although we prefer the S in Eyeshot to remain uncapitalized, your unnecessary capitalization has not influenced our reading of your work. And, with regard to your previous publications, if you would send a copy of the "St. Louis Business Journal" to 650 Humboldt St #2, Brooklyn, NY, 11222, it would be appreciated. Enough preliminaries, let's get on with this response, but let's do it slowly, maximize the suspense. I liked the way, especially toward the end in the boat, the language is cleaner than in the beginning, in which it seemed like you modified every noun:

For example: *rosy pink blush light — purpled darkness — shy sky — the hem of its nighttime dress — slowly exposing a flaming, skinned knee — low moaning hum of the highway — the faint drone — the bent gray cross of it — a grape juice heaven — billowing trail*

You're trying to make the reader see more, but you're getting in the way of what's seen. You seem to do much better with the narrative parts (the fishing boat) than the descriptive parts (see above). Good luck with your book—and remember to send the journal.

You're from the 718, so you get a lower level of scrutiny. But I just can't roll with violence written violently — can't hang with it well enough to care — or dig thru the sentence surface. And I'm not into bottles of Jack and Bud, not in stories at least. Sorry. We also received a negative comment about misogyny in a few stories we've posted, and those were abstractions in which no women were explicitly choked.

As the Human League once wrote, keep feeling 'fatuation, bodies moving, something, something. Although November displays its misty final days, with everything decaying as though by beauty's design, we blossom. And now, whilst we're all a-blossomed, we'd really be pissed if we dissuaded you from infatuation, especially at such a pivotal time in our relationship, what with the winter coming on and squirrels of the world like us must gather nuts as we may. This is the exciting time. Before first touch. Before we mix files on various drives and you send words that I format and (I blush) upload them for all the world to see. But, we hope that this stumblingly shy, red-earr'd rejection will not quench your fire. We prefer when suitors send beautiful sentences set into paragraphs — the poesy need not be quite poesy, or it need be poesy that knocks us on our apple-orbed asses, to find its place upon the Eyeshot screen. Not that what you send offends, just that it's not quite what we're looking for, which, perchance, five days reading the archives would reveal. But don't let any of this belie the fact of our infatuation, or really, your infatuation, since we have never seen you, and despite admiring depth, humor, and "puhsenility," we're all about surfaces, darling.

    Eyeshot's Aphrodisiacal Chalice of Ecstatic Oysters and Spiced Cider

No thanks. But thanks.

Hi. Thanks for sending this. But I wonder why you set it at the dentist? Anyway, I'd be interested in this if a simple visit to the dentist were presented as a self-consciously overblown allegory for aesthetic conformity and/or conformity to American society, but that's not really what I sense going on here. So instead I'll flash my gap-toothed smile and says thanks and sorry and good luck.

The story you three sent is pretty straight, yet telling a tale that's hard to follow and seemingly arbitrary. What I'm saying is that the overall tone and characterization and setting calls for a simply told STORY, I think, and you all sort of roam along without a constant voice or narrative momentum in command, which makes it hard to read and enjoy. But that's just my opinion, of course. I'm also sick, hungover, and on too much NyQuil, which you once could drink an overdose of without getting horrible stomach cramps. Transparency is a hot word now and so I reveal my disarrayed accounting books. Doing so lets the three of you see someone on the other side of the screen. I feel like the skin on my face has taken on the consistency of one of those huge slices of stone-white rye bread from the Polish grocery store around the corner from me. Last night until way too late there wasn't much of a distance between myself and what I saw but now I need a good submission to bridge a jagged gap that might just be a projection of the fissure in my head. As I read what you all sent, certain stylistic things made my readerly self plunge to the death, too many sentences with that I'm gonna add weight to this sentence simply by ending with a comma and then a final weighty word or phrase, like "unfulfilled." I'm not gonna give specific examples—what if all the examples I picked were by the same person? You see the danger, the complications, the dread of responding to a collaboration like this. So, look, thanks very much for sending this to us, considering all the sites out there, and I apologize for not having much to say that's really nice. The content needs to match the collaborative process more for it to work, I think. But others might like it better than someone who's quick to admit to liking things a little more idiosyncratic. And that's sort of the issue with the collaboration, right? How to constrain one's voice or harmonize it to match those of others so there's a coherent or at least non-distracting tone—I wonder what it'd be like with three stylists, three writers with drastically unique voices? I wonder if you could get three such writers to do it? What I don't like about the collaborative idea is this leveling of voices, since what I respond to most in writing is voice, use of language, etc. If it's an academic exercise in harmony, I'm not really interested in it. Which leads me to writing programs and the homogenizing toward "the ideal" of some workshopped fiction etc etc etc. Anyway, just beginning to fight my way out of a bright warm Sunday spent sick, hungover, dreading. Wish I could say something better than I have — I apologize again if I've been too harsh. Hope I haven't made your starry eyes well up.

Sorry for the spareness of the reply, but plagiarists get less than special consideration.

You need to mention at least four people we know for automatic inclusion. Unfortunately, you only mentioned three. Laugh Riot is not a requirement for submissions, but we do look for a little something your submission seems to lack. The story's almost an essay, which is fine if the piece is written semi-ecstatically and overintellectually — but your thing's written in a style that doesn't do it for us. It's easy to read, understandable and all that, but I guess we look for more performance. Your submission makes too much sense, I think, and on a sentence-to-sentence basis, it wobbles a little. Don't send something you dusted off about dead people. Take some chances, write something new, something you've never done before that you don't think could get accepted anywhere else, then send it here. That's the advice section of the rejection note. Sorry, but thanks for submitting. I hope you kick some ass, trace the bruises, and send them here.

Hi. Thanks for submitting. It's great that you'd like to put this on Eyeshot. But it can't happen. Not with this story. Would you like to know why? Because there's not much of a story and the writing's not particularly original or funny or mean or anything. That is what I think. Do you hate me now? You shouldn't. I don't hate you because I didn't want to post your story. The story exists outside of you. You are not your story. You can take what I say and think about it, or cry, or tell me to piss off. All are acceptable. Or you can ignore me. Whatever. By which I mean to say, thanks for submitting and please send something again if you ever recover from the crushing blow this rejection served to your artistic ego.

Eyeshot's Supermean Ego Extractor

Hi. At first I thought this was written by a German and was all excited to post it! The language was terribly off, but in a great way, and it was about America to boot! So I thought I'd post it unedited and it'd be cool that way. Then I realized the voice was Japanese and I had to change it in my head from the German. Then I started thinking that it wasn't authentically wrong, but a contrived accent. Then I started to get a little bored with it. Then I skimmed along and saw that you're an expat American. Then I hit reply and began writing this rejection note. Then I tried to be nice. I typed things like thanks for submitting and good luck with your book and please try again. Then I ended the message, typing my name and saying that I'm the editor of the site to which you submitted, but I tweaked the site's name to something like "Eyeshot's Axis-Power Accent Mistake."

I'd like this more if the additive weren't crack. It doesn't have to be crack, does it? Of all the possible things existing in the world and all the possible things you could imagine the kids might add to the specially concocted beverage they make for their grandparents when they visit in the nursing home, the inclusion of the word "crack," much like the addition of the word "monkeys," only makes readers think that what they're reading is now "supposed to be funny." Crack isn't all that funny, not really. There are substitutes. Nonsensical substitutes. Other additives. There must be. So if you recast this with something other than crack as the additive, I'd like to see it — otherwise...

OK! Stop a sec. You've submitted eight pieces in one day. And they've all been rejected. How does that make you feel? Maybe you should work a little harder on one or two things. You seem to get an idea and think the idea itself is worthwhile. You should work a little harder. Concentrate. Give the idea a context that makes what's funny about it come to life. Please don't send more of these little jokes and lists. They're not funny. Particularly the spam thing. Not funny at all. Sorry. Also, you shouldn't submit more than one thing at a time. Editors get pissed. I'm hungover and homebound on a beautiful day and there's nothing much else I can do, so it's been a pleasure responding to these as quickly as I can. If I step outside, I bet all of New York is frolicking in the sun, parks are lousy with the semi-exposed limbs of supermodel wannabes from as far away as Metuchen, tourists wearing designer sunglasses have come from all over the world to soak in Ground Zero, yet here I am existentially exposed to the devastation you've wrought upon my poor little defenseless Eyeshot Inbox. Late last night I was boundless energy personified, relentless thirst, desire, awareness, alive in an endless city of funny smart pretty eagle-winged adolescents in their late twenties I somehow didn't hate, but now the world seems reduced to you and me. Listen, if someone accepts any of these, do not trust that source. You've got some work to do. You've got good ideas, but you've got to build little houses for them to run around in, get me? Good. Treat what you're doing like your children, not flies that you catch for a minute, rattle, then send off into the world.

Eyeshot's Bloodshot Brains

I like fragments but these don't quite do it for me. Please don't respond saying something about hoping an extra-sharp greased ostrich beak rammed in my bum would "do it for me." Send something else please.

Hi. I like the formal thing of the outgoing message, but it pretty quickly seems like a contrivance because you include dialogue with quotation marks, formal contrivances of fiction etc... if it were all one voice-driven rant I'd have liked it better, especially if the voice mentioned WHY it was leaving such a long rant-type message on the answering machine. Also, the whole-catching-lover-with-friend thing is grounds for immediate rejection—we get a few of those a week. If the voice caught the lover with something else, something impossible, caught her having sex with a hot-air balloon flying around her bedroom, using an impossible object (a 15-foot trumpet) on her, etc, then we'd have something. So... I can't accept it, but if you ever revise it, I'd like to see it... And if not, thanks for the submission and please send more soon.

Eyeshot's Sad Smoke Signal

Thank you for submitting this story about motherfucking pretentious Nazi hamster fuckers. I liked the dialogue but when you got all expository-like about malls, I lost interest. Sorry. This could be a good story if it were shorter and more controlled, but you probably just pasted it from somewhere else—it's probably about Molly Ringwald, right?

What is this character doing out at the bar with the boys and why should anyone follow him through a night of mojitos and glances and all that for 3390 words just to learn that the guy has a girlfriend or a wife or a female something in his bed? Why? What's your intention? What's the point? Is the surprise at the end enough to make the reading worthwhile? There are some nice parts and the dialogue's smooth and it's all rendered realistically and naturally but when the ending comes, it seems at once tacked on and yet also the crux to the story. Dunno. It's weird here right now: you have a NYC cellphone number so if you're reading this today, Friday afternoon, you know it's humid or just sorta weird out like it wants to rain but won't and I was out too late at a bar that serves mojitos and has good free live music in a tiny narrow room in back and then another place with a giant shimmering camel on the wall where the bathroom lines tend to move way too slowly after a certain hour but the music is perfect (lots of Buffalo Springfield last night, and at one point Beefheart's "Kandy Korn") and my head's sore and I came home to an empty bed (alas, the joys of having a long-distance girlfriend in Iowa), and I see how it would have been a different night if all along I knew my bed were occupied. But I can't post this, although I'd be glad to look at anything else you'd like to send, maybe something considerably shorter?

Eyeshot's Crushed Cousin of the Julep

Thanks for submitting this. It's a nice story that, I think, serves its purpose and probably does what you'd like it to do. It's a meditation-type thing that reads really well and naturally and seems to have some basic merit that way. But it's not for us. If you read the pieces on Eyeshot, you'll see that most of them are a little more agitated or churning or unquiet or nervous or scatological or juvenile or free-associative et cetera. I think the sensibility of this story is too mature, too solid, too trustworthy for us. Again, I like it fine and think it does its job but it's sort of like a collection of impressions that don't leave a lasting one — that's all I can say... It could probably be published most anywhere: good luck.

Eyeshot's 4-Second Memory

I liked the way it started but the words were kind of like passing clouds after a while, and I wasn't paying attention to them as well as I should have, and as more clouds passed it got more and more overcast until I couldn't see the words because I'd clicked the reply button and started writing this response. It's a good idea but doesn't seem like it's executed with the vibrancy and urgency or whatever that's required to keep people scrolling all the way down their screens, know what I mean?

So you're in India? That's amazing. That's great. I love that. It's fantastic when people from all over the world submit. Or maybe you just have this Indian e-mail address and actually live in Edison, New Jersey? Well, because I wanted to accept this, thinking that it'd be cool to add to the collection of non-American, non-Brooklynites on the site, I was willing to give it the benefit of the doubt, but after a while I wasn't inspired to keep scrolling down, although I kept on, eventually making it all the way down to the nubile Brahmin girls (yaozah!). But I can't accept the submission. It seemed too slow and sort of plodding for the site (for the internet in general where attention spans are three seconds long). I liked the way you used the language and found the cultural things semi-interesting, but also familiar and not so riveting.

Eyeshot's See-Through Sari

No. No. No. No. No. I'm not finding this funny. I am unequivocally rejecting this piece. Please do not send revisions. If you ever send me something else about Steven the Gay Man and his little tray of freaking whatever, I will delete the message unread. This is all especially disappointing since I read something you wrote today on uber.nu that I thought was funny, but this stuff you're sending me is not so funny. How do you think it makes me feel when you send your good stuff elsewhere and your unfunny stuff here? I apologize but I have to maintain stringent standards since my father reads the site each day with the strictest possible scrutiny and lets me know, depending on his enjoyment of each piece, whether he will continue funding my monkish life devoted to online literary pursuits for that day. If he likes what I post he sends via PayPal $5 and I use this to buy wild-rice tempeh, jumbo eggs, and a Vanilla Coke. So no, no, no, no, no, a thousand times no.

REJECTION LETTERS FROM THE EYESHOT OUTBOX

Thank you. We have had certain issues with prostitution in the past, however, and would prefer to avoid the issue. Sorry.

Eyeshot's Editorial Lapjack

I just printed up your submission and read it. It's 10:15 PM. I was out too late last night. I warn you that I may not have been in the best shape to read a piece like this one. I am operating this website in a somewhat impaired condition. Whenever energetic and fresh, I'm out in the world, running around, diluting overwhelming energy and freshness with lagers until I reach a point where I feel not so energetic or fresh and the next day know I'll feel crappy enough to effectively operate Eyeshot. What follows therefore is my reckless response: the style is good, but I don't feel there's enough drive to compel web readers to scroll down, not even through the first few paragraphs. There's something enticingly musty about the piece, almost librarian, if you can use that word as an adjective. It felt like a rainy day game of Clue. But I was not really able to apprehend it, which may have been your intention, since you subtitled it a "post-apprehension murder mystery." I'll admit that I don't really know what happened. Even in my somewhat impaired state, I think I should be able to make my way through it and pick up on the basic happenings, the goings on: I'd like to post things that momentarily clear the eyes of the bleary. Maybe what you're trying to do is too subtle for me now, and with a few cups of coffee in the morning, I'd love it, but I don't think so. I'll go with my intuition, which is telling me to thank you and apologize and say things about regret. And also to insist that you send something else for consideration, since we like the form but not so much the content. And also that we would love to be included among your list of places where you've published pieces.

Eyeshot's Self-Inflicted Headwound

I like the formal endnote thing, but the content's a downer. Suicide's a downer, isn't? It used to be, is it still? Do you know why everyone's sending stuff about suicide? What the hell? People must be trying to kill other people off? People must think that other people waking up/drinking coffee who are more or less happy would like to read really short "experimentally" constructed fictional bits about people who've killed themselves. Do you know why? Apparently people must want to read such short bits about people who have offed themselves? It's weird, all these people wanting to read such things! And I say, no — no, you people out there — you can't get what you want! You'll have to look elsewhere if you'd like to read such things, although I don't think other sites have anything like what you've sent, which maybe is good, since maybe they'll accept it if you send it to them. Unfortunately, I am currently unable to validate your choice of vocation. Perhaps the skills you learn at your MFA program will do some good when you take a job as a professional copywriter? I don't know. But you will write more and more and send everywhere and soon, in a year or two decades, all will be fine. Persistence. Patience. Endurance. Resubmittance soon.

Eyeshot's Suicide Ain't No Solution

If the lion and the mouse were eaten by a giant swooping robot bird at the end and then excreted upon an American tourist/ Hemingway fan hunting elephants, maybe, just maybe this would have a chance, but instead it's what it is: a fable that's a little wimpy, a little trite, but otherwise nicely done and probably quite acceptable at sites that don't require the sudden appearance of swooping robot birds or the infiltration of everything at the end by Israeli secret police (I stole that last bit from Mark Leyner). Thanks for submitting. Maybe read a few more pieces in the archive before submitting again, which would be nice. Also please note that we have responded within an hour of submission, thereby enabling you to send this piece out again in the same evening, as though none of this had ever happened.

Eyeshot's Swooping Robot Editor

Some parts of this seem translated from the original French or German, and I bet you read a lot of theorists and philosophers and such, right? If so, maybe the general flow/spirit/tone of your language might perchance benefit, especially in terms of getting something on Eyeshot, from a little more unpredictable forward propulsion, i.e., "swerve." You present a nearly academic take on things, which is fine, but I'd prefer it to seem unlike something you might hand in for a grade. I like the idea of what you sent, but I think I'd prefer if the formal execution, especially for something about Dana Plato, were more performative, virtuosic, far-flung, a touch more incomprehensible and weird, like if the whole thing seemed like a serious comparison of the works of Dana Plato and the philosopher but really wound up being about their shared love for eating PlayDoh. What I mean is: all the ideas can get into the piece but wrapped in other clothes.

I'd like what you sent a little more if it were rapped. It seems like a poem from which you extracted the line breaks, which, of course, according to the submission guidelines, is recommended. I like a lot of the language, the general instinct of it. But the sensibility, that sort of perspective on "the urban" you present, isn't something I want to post on Eyeshot. Cities, at least good ones like NYC, deserve more generosity and particularity than what you give them. Stories shouldn't reduce the complexity of cities to descriptions perpetuating outdated stereotypes. If you were writing some updated pseudo noir stuff featuring Raymond Chandler with an iPod and a Jeter jersey, I'd get it, but that's not the case with this. Times Square isn't the home of peep-show stripper perversions anymore. So much more is going on, right? For example, the suburbanification of cities. A bike lane down the middle of the Williamsburg Bridge. Transformation of old elevated train tracks in Chelsea into a park above street level. So maybe I'd prefer more details, descriptions, specific reference. Or maybe I misinterpreted the story. Anyway. Send something else!

You misspelled the word "about" in the first sentence, and there's sloppiness throughout the first paragraph, plus I wasn't totally interested or compelled to scroll, since I was, as I said, distracted by the misspelling and sloppiness. Now you might think that harping on misspelling and sloppiness is lame, and I might agree with you, but I would also say that it alerts me to the fact that you haven't spent much time revising the fucker or polishing it or even REREADING it once or twice to attend to your copyediting chores. And since you didn't take the time to reread and clean the fucker up, I'll admit to not taking the time to read the fucker all the way through. Sorry. But I'm glad you decided to submit and maybe if you want to work on this one or another a little more and resend it, I'd be more than glad to give it a good look. Otherwise, piss off. (Insert devilish-grin emoticon.)

Eyeshot's White-Sky Day

I like the basic situation and all, but I think it went on too long, and I didn't laugh out loud, the sole requirement for accepting pieces that seem intended to make people laugh. For Eyeshot, I'd maybe suggest making the steps of the numbered-list thing get progressively improbable until they really have nothing at all to do with the main subject (dog barking) at all. For example, #10 would be: "Buy some shoe polish and apply it to an aluminum baseball bat then see if it slides down the steps better than a traditional wooden bat, corked or not with shredded lasagna noodles or chocolate coins." Etc, etc. (I did like the inclusion of the number 37, however.)

First of all I think this is just too damn long for the web. It'd probably do better at a print journal. Second, I read the opening sections with the three characters and enjoyed them somewhat, but not enough to suggest you break the story up or that we run it as a serialized thing—although I liked that one of the characters is from the planet Clog. But I didn't really feel like the story kept me from being distracted by the loud-mouthed dickwads on the street who are currently screaming and blasting 50 Cent. I think they might be responsible for my failure to get sucked into the story, or it could be the story's fault that they weren't tuned out? I have no idea which. They also have an old rottweiler whose brain has grown too big for its skull and so it barks a lot. Let that be a lesson to everyone. Anyway. Thanks for sending this and maybe try sending it to print mags. And also try sending something else that's considerably shorter. Thanks again and sorry.

Eyeshot's Editorial Alien

Thank you for sending this thing about goat milk. I liked the chain of tastes at first wherein milk tastes like sperm that tastes like IHOP but then it gets confused with the bit about how IHOP tastes like rape?! It's too random and potentially offensive without offering the game-winning salvation of a legit LOL. It didn't really do much (entertain, make me laugh) to make me wanna post it. But very little time has been wasted. Submit it elsewhere now and it'll be like this never happened. Thanks again for sending, and sorry.

Eyeshot's Coco Milk Squirt

I know that area of town, around 53rd and 1st—there's a big Starbucks across from a bagel store, I think. A few diners. A nice pub where I go if I'm early for a little writing group I go to over there once a week at the not particularly ostentatious apartment of a top-notch semi-surrealist writer who was described to me at first as a "billionairess." Not that that matters. This was very readable. I was able to read it all the way through. It was clear. I liked the confrontation with the drunk, how the narrator came off sort of shy or beaten and sick of it but not necessarily too able to talk down a table-standing drunk. But after the diner scene, I didn't particularly go along on the bus ride way up to the Royal Tennenbaums' part of town or the intimation that she slit her throat—a little too melodramatic for good ole Eyeshot. But as I said, the story reads well and you should be able to get it accepted somewhere else, I'm sure. Thanks again for submitting and please send something again soonish.

Eyeshot's Falling Sky

It seems like you've provided two slices of bread and the whole point of the story is to induce the thought of the lunch meat in the reader, which is a cool thing—the fact that the woman killed herself. OK. So. Then. What? It's a fine little short, but I think, as with your other submissions recently, I'd prefer a little more realistic life, descriptions. This guy in the trench coat, the subway straps. They don't feel real—as I've said before, I have an aversion to things that opt for a sort of "traditional real" or a "clichéd real" compared to a hyper-real or surreal reality. Not sure if that makes sense? What I mean is: I'd like to see something that seems less explicitly like a sandwich.

The first one reminded me of Kafka's meditations, the one about when you're despairing on a rainy night you should walk through the city and knock on the door of a friend. This one involved elephants and subways, nicely, and explicitly mentioned Cambridge, which discolored it for me since I used to live in Jamaica Plain (long live the path around the pond, Arnold Arboretum, the Brendan Behan) but have never been much of a fan of Cambridge or Boston in general, mainly for personal reasons that have little to do with the city's infrastructure etc, which actually, come to think of it, isn't wonderful. In general, when I lived there, I was sure that whatever brings about the end of the world (or at least the end of the human race) will be discovered in a lab at M.I.T., Harvard, or a biotech thereabouts. With a Boston-inspired apocalypse in mind, I nevertheless liked the first story except for the bit about Cambridge, which really, beside my personal thing, limited associations among elephant and subway and city more than extended them. The second one, I can't quite remember: was it about unrequited love? The pathologically hopeful guy, the girl, the marriage, the baby, the joke about smothering the child and winding up in jail for 99 years. I liked that one, too, although it didn't really mesh with the first thing that much, meaning the first one cooly focused reality and then the second was a game and therefore disappointing, a little too whimsical? The third one I can't remember, not even five minutes after reading it. What was it again? (I peeked.) Right. Something involving laundry and dishes, and then winding up in jail. Mundane and clever, like something someone sitting outside Au Bon Pain might scribble on their laptop. (Insert evil emoticon.). So: if the third one were much stronger, if the middle one were shorter, and if the first one didn't mention Cambridge and had a more interesting title—anything at all—I would accept one or all of them. But instead I think I'm gonna thank you for submitting and state that the first one has a pretty good chance of getting accepted somewhere, but not here, not now.

Why call this flash fiction? Or sudden fiction? Those are silly things to call something you wrote, right? Regardless, I don't think this bit of writing is right for Eyeshot. The length is good, but it involves childhood and we're trying to stay out of that area—but the good news is that there currently exist eight dozen websites willing to accept nicely rendered stories like this and so you should have no trouble finding a home for this one. We realize we're like that neurotic kid who runs away from you because your shoelaces are white. Sorry. We get lots of well-written submissions involving childhood, but we like it odd and quick and rangy and fun. Thanks again for submitting—you'll have no trouble posting this elsewhere.

Thanks for submitting. So I think I like what you sent. I like the language of it. But I don't think it's really right for Eyeshot — how would it be right? I guess if the whole take on it were more a prank, less honest, more absurd — it would start as it does and then its pop-culture examples would swerve into absurdities, not mentioning anything anyone ever heard of — instead of Kate Hudson, it would be about the narrator's experience discovering the nascent Hasidic/talking fish video porn business, sort of suggesting pop-culture (talking fish thing = recent news item), working everything at an obtuse angle — not that what you sent is bad or stupid or anything at all like that — it's fine, just I think I'd like to post things that don't make as much sense, that aren't quite as sane. The gist of what you sent is more or less understood early on and so there's opportunity to play with the reader's expectation, if you'd like. Good luck with it — I'm sure you'll have no trouble getting it posted somewhere, someday. Eyeshot ain't that place today.

Eyeshot's Snobby Doorknob

Hi — the thing on the site right now involves a blowjob and some cunnilingus and all, but the joke of the first part is the G-rated mention of late-period REM. I like the way you seem to really enjoy the fellatio in your submission, but I'm not so sure how much I like the submissive aspects of it.

I liked the basic readability and the flow but not the gay stereotype stuff especially since it didn't turn out that his brother was gay or that he in fact was gay and then the bit with the affair and the promise to off the lover felt super-thin and unrealistic and fictional — in the fake sense — but mainly it all seemed underdone as far as a "story" goes — I really liked the detail about the boysenberry martini with a hint of lemon or whatever but disliked the fact that the waiter "swishes" — that's lazy writing, as opposed to the martini detail. Also, please realize that this is just the opinion of one dude in Brooklyn drinking coffee and reading the submissions that came in last night when he was at the William T. Vollmann slideshow lecture thing for his 3000 page, 23-year-old effort about the history of violence, a book or an artifact really, that sort of makes me want the site to do a little more than just bat about sexual-preference stereotypes? Last night, Vollmann suggested that one solution to our country's current international problems would be to elect someone else president and then scapegoat the shit out of Bush so the world hates him instead of the U.S — that's a very good idea. Maybe that can also apply to this rejection note, which is long and quickly returned and absolutely not at all a form letter and is intended as both critique and embrace. So please don't hate me for typing more in this note than you did in your story! Oh yeah, and send something else if you'd like, ya poof.

Eyeshot's Flamboyant Testicle

Thanks but no thanks, Mr. Garcia. I wish you well this season with the 49ers. My friends still mourn the death of your father.

Sorry for the slight delay there — was busy, had to organize and listen to and look up the value of some of the 700 or so 45 RPM records I just bought at a NJ thrift store for $10. Eyeshot might have a rare record store component sometime soon! Stacks of Stax records, some worth more than $10 themselves. So I've been doing that, procrastinating from freelance work and the "non-profitable" writing I usually do to procrastinate as well — and thankfully this delay has allowed for you to send a revision, which I just read. Here's what I think: The title reminds me of that famous Barthelme story, "Some of Us Have Been Threatening Our Friend Colby" — being reminded of that is a good thing. But then I think in general, I'd prefer for this one to be a ton more absurd, with the same basic structure, but instead of "manic depression, schizophrenia, etc" you would use that list to throw in a few semi-imaginative jokes — same with the way the main dude in your story died — pills? — it could have been anything, right? That's the point, I think — nearly every detail could be anything — what you include seems believable but randomly selected, so if the goal of this thing is to amuse people — it's not really attempting to "enlighten" or anything, right? It's not really an informative allegory about how treating weird kids weirdly causes them to off themselves down the road. So, assuming you're trying to entertain, make people laugh etc, I think the easiest way to achieve that goal is through surreal juxtaposition, the creation of expectation and then bursting it — but this creates and then extends the expectation, setting things up but not knocking them down, yeah? Not that I think what you sent sucks or anything — I thought it read well and was "amusing," if not laugh out loud funny — when people submit funny things I tend to only post them if I laugh out loud at least once, a reasonable barometer for judging submissions, since there's no decision really — either you hear yourself laugh or not, and chances are if I laughed at least one other person might laugh, too, esp. since I tend not to laugh at things that are intended to be funny because I'm on guard against what the writer wants me to do. And so I think I'd suggest that maybe you play with it and resubmit it or send it elsewhere and hope whoever reads it is more easily amused. Anyway — thanks again for submitting — sorry I'm not going to accept this one as it is right now — but I'm sure I'll accept something else later.

Eyeshot's Nest of Salt

This is great. But I'm not going to accept it. Actually, I lied. It's not great. Jennifer Aniston is married to Brad Pitt. I mean, really! Even I know that. I didn't laugh once. There's some funny potential somewhere in there but I don't think you really found it. Maybe if the descriptions had less to do with anything at all related to smoking it'd all be funnier. Or maybe if I were quicker to laugh, more an idiot, on more pills? However.

I like this, but I'm not going to post it. It's really nicely subtle, but maybe a little too much so for Eyeshot. Not that subtlety is bad or that nothing on Eyeshot is subtle. Just that it seems subtle in a way that makes me think that I have to read it a few times again to really get it. But I didn't really feel the text was loaded so much or I didn't quite feel so engaged with it when I read it the first time. That sort of readerly engagement is really important online. Otherwise, people take advantage of the internet's ADD-inducing effect and zone out and flip elsewhere. But I do think it will quite possibly find a home at some other site where the editors are more patient and imagine the site's readers are patient, too. What can I say but thank you and sorry!

Had some trouble with this since I didn't really believe it. When men or women write in the opposite sex's first-person voice, so-called "cross-gender writing," as a reader I tend to have it too closely in mind that I'm reading a story, so the bar regarding suspension of disbelief is raised, and then also as a writer you have to prove to the reader that the narrator is a man by showing something only men would know—you have to flash the secret code by which disbelief is suspended. Not that men shouldn't write as women or women as men but just that I feel like doing so creates an obstacle in my head as a reader the writer must overcome. I have no trouble believing third-person POV of course, but a first-person crossover voice, not so much. Maybe that's just me, but I'm also the sole member of the Eyeshot editorial board. So: here you're writing as a male sexual predator, a date raper, but it didn't feel to me like a particular character as much as a stereotype, a composite nasty guy. I also couldn't read it closely enough to know whether you were playing with all this, satirizing it, and I honestly didn't make it to the end. That's not the critique you want to hear, or the reaction, but I'm sure you'll keep kicking it since you obviously have the talent (I liked the language in the last one better—more playful)—so thanks again for sending this and I apologize—please realize my comments only apply to bits of text I read around 10:24 on Thursday night EST, nearly finished with a pint of wine—that the comments above have nothing to do with you or your family or the state of California—so send me something else maybe?

I really liked the idea of coming back and choosing to be a giant mushroom. A very good idea that filled me with expectation for what you'd come up with. But then there were sheep. OK. And anthrax. OK. So I guess I would have liked to have heard more about being a giant mushroom, perhaps the history of previous tenants or your plans for the place or maybe how you were sending out spores in certain directions at certain times to influence certain happenings? Like it'd be cool if, after reading about the giant mushroom, I walked outside and figured there's a giant mushroom under the streets of Brooklyn right now and that's why the traffic light changed at a time when no car would have killed me. Or something. So I'm basically saying it's a cool idea but you should think about it and work on it and revise it and work on it some more. Cool? Cool.

Oh shit you're from New Zealand! How cool?! So I like what you sent. Think it's a fine parody of academic writing, but it was a little too difficult for me to get through — sorry. But send something else. It would be my pleasure to post something by someone in New Zealand.

Eyeshot's Eyeless Monocle

I'm from New Jersey too — I liked how this started but it didn't really seem like anything more, it just sort of petered out and died. NJ has a tradition of amazing highways and writers — it is your job to work with the industry of those who laid down the Turnpike and Parkway, and mix the pavement with the creativity of Auster, William Carlos Williams, Whitman, Ginsberg, even Jonathan Ames! But thanks again for submitting and please send something else whenever.

Eyeshot's Route 206er

Hi — please don't refer to your fiction as "flash"— why do that? Who made up that modifier? Why adopt it? Anyway — I don't think this submission is right for Eyeshot. There were no alligators in it. Maybe if you exchanged the hail for alligators and the CEO for a baseball bat, we'd have something, but as it is, with neither alligator nor baseball bat, we cannot offer acceptance. Sorry. But thanks for submitting and good luck with this elsewhere!

Eyeshot's Aluminum Crocodile

Hi — thanks for sending something again — I think this is a pretty good traditional-type narrative that would probably have a very good chance at most traditional-type websites and probably a few print journals, too. But it's not right for Eyeshot because there are no radioactive cows in it. Nor one mention of a single bison made of recycled paper products and very, very dangerous plastic. Sorry. But thanks for sending again — I'm sure you'll have better luck elsewhere.

Please realize that Eyeshot is an online thing, available on a medium wherein people's attention spans are widely known to be limited, hence, where something like Will Ratblood's ball-touching spiel goes over very well — it's partly about the simplicity, the length, the humor — what you've sent twice, while humorous, didn't necessarily make me laugh out loud either time and just seems a little too long and a convoluted way to point out southern media-related racial stereotypes. I think you nailed Mr. Morehouse's voice, but I'd have liked to have seen a lot less of this — it's not something that I think really needs to go on and on, since the joke of it, or whatever its "special value" is, doesn't really evolve in a totally surprising/ interesting/unexpected way, but I honestly can't say I read every word with anything approaching extreme concentration. But I thank you for submitting (AGAIN) and hope you send SOMETHING ELSE sometime soon, maybe something a little shorter?

Learn to spell FELLATIO! I'm not going to post this because it's not funny at all. But thanks for sending it.

I really liked the one about throwing balls through halos. I suggest you take that idea and write a story about someone who can actually see halos and throws things through them, etc. It'd be great. What you sent is pretty good, but I don't think I'm going to post it on Eyeshot. I had a little trouble getting into some of the earlier bits and although I liked the tone and general instinct, there was something about these that seemed not quite right for the site. That doesn't mean they suck or anything — I'm sure one of the "Kindred" sites linked to Eyeshot will respond more favorably, if considerably slower.

Hey — I read this two days ago and was very undecided — there was a lot that I liked about it, though I thought it was a little long for Eyeshot — I didn't mind the jerking off and I liked the girl and all — but I couldn't decide on it — usually I know right away, so not knowing either way was odd — it's only happened once before — the other time I chose to accept it — so this time, I think I'll let you know as honestly as I can that I really had no idea what to do and flipped a coin. It came up on the wrong side and so I'm not going to post this — it's not really as arbitrary as it seems, since if the submission made me want to accept it more I would simply have accepted it without resorting to coins — I wanted you to have a chance, but alas, the coin has spoken—send something else soon though — as I said, I liked what you sent, if not enough not to resort to the flip of the coin. Let this be an exaggerated lesson in the arbitrariness of acceptance and decline.

Eyeshot's Indecisive Incision

Yo Iowa City! The past year or so I've been spending a little time out there now and again since my GF lives there. Maybe I've seen you. Are you blond and fresh-faced and tend to only wear clothing that's black and gold with the word "Iowa" appearing either across chest or buttocks? So I like the story, although I don't think it's a story — it seems more like the beginning of a really great story, but as it is, it seems too much like not enough — I liked it, but I'm thinking about it in terms of the site, and I think it might have started too slowly for the web, inducing maybe too many thoughts in my head about *Reality Bites*. I liked the dialogue, the car bit, the italicized teal, but then it ended — it seems a good start for something better than what it is right now. Anyway — thanks again and sorry for not posting this — maybe try something else?

Eyeshot's Appreciator of
The Sanctuary's Pizza &
Panchero's Burritos

We don't post stories that are set in Hawaii, include psychedelics, or kill dogs. It's really that simple. Well, actually, there's more to it. The way it started with the botany class, I thought it'd lead to something more funny, but I think I got distracted in the middle part — there's this dog and this mushroom and so the dog's consumption of the mushroom is inevitable. Okay. But. I don't know. The dog should have maybe shat out a mushroom slurry after he ate it, and that's how the guy got his botany job, because his dog shat a super-psychedelic mushroom slurry and the hippie administrators at Evergreen gave him the "job" in exchange for a heaping spoonful of his dog's trippy shit. But instead, you killed the dog, which is something you should never do unless absolutely necessary!!! Sorry — but thanks again for submitting. And I hope you're able to send this one out elsewhere tonight.

Eyeshot's Canine of Cannabis

This is like a joke fable that blurred my attention after five lines. Sorry but thanks for sending it and good luck!

Thanks for sending this! It starts out well and is very smooth and nicely written, but I think it's better off for print than the web. It requires more readerly patience than readers online can currently provide? It's more like something you want to cozy up with in bed or take to quiet private locations where you read with your pants at your ankles. Readers online are strapped to desktops, their patience limited by a combo of limitless scroll and the ability at any second to access fantasy sports or porn. If you're a huge e-lit enthusiast, it's probably better off on a site that's a little more traditional than Eyeshot. I might have missed them, but I don't think there were any talking animals in this one, nor were there clouds that ejaculate bluebirds and redbirds and hummingbirds, no highways deciding to take to the skies, no allusions to bad TV or good literature, no unpronounceable words, not nearly enough three-letter words, and not nearly enough words that stand for colors that look like sounds that sound like smells. By which I mean I think this story is good and would be happier if its final resting place were a little saner than one of the slots reserved for silliness over at the ole Eyeshot. But thanks again for submitting and please send something else whenever.

Eyeshot's Pre-Conception Fatality

I really like how this started out and I liked the pace and dialogue of it. But then the story dissolved—like you set up something that then disappeared. I'd suggest you work on this a while and maybe see why you wanted to write it and see how those characters you set up and the great tension of the two dads moving off the backyard would play out over time. Anyway, again, I really like how it started, but then it seemed like you were thinking more about restricting word count than expanding the story.

Hello Melbourne! I really like your name and I like your tone and the instinct of what you sent, but I think I'd maybe have liked it more if it were maybe a little more unified or didn't state an idea and then trail off a little. So. Thanks for submitting and please send again whenever. We're all about representing Australia!

Eyeshot's Simpson's Booting

Thanks again for sending something. It's snowing in NYC and citrus is what it's about when it's snowing, mass doses of orange juice and oranges and grapefruit until you yourself are tropical paradise while the weather outside is frightful. Such is the sole benefit of being a work-from-home freelancer. For some reason, perhaps because the thing on the site right now is over-the-top sexy, three people have recently submitted sexy food submissions! Very strange! And I like this one more than the other two, but I'm not going to accept it, since I guess I'd like for the food-sex cliché thing to set something else up — y'know all those movies like *Like Water for Chocolate* and *The Cook, The Thief, His Wife, and Her Lover,* wherein the gourmand and the voluptuary (that's a Homer Simpson reference) get all intertwined, opens a can of expectation for the reader, and obvious expectations can always be played with, right? So I'd like to thank you again and say that I liked the instinct and intention of what you sent, but I'd have liked it more if it used its momentum to undercut the reader's expectation, to make the reader laugh or smile as the piece went off somewhere no one would easily anticipate.

Hey Dayton! Thanks for calling us kick ass. Although we often post misspelled rhyming love poetry by a young Egyptian soldier, we rarely accept poetry by native speakers. Sorry.

Eyeshot's Oberlin Ohio

I'd maybe accept this if it were all about little known *Kama Sutra* positions for sleeping with your "panther," instead of "partner." I misread the first line as "Lie sideways in bed, with your back turned to your panther" and thought that would be an amazing thing to post if it were a lot like this one, nonsexual and stodgy, but about sleeping with your panther instead of your "partner." Panthers. Panthers. That'll be all I think about until the Yankees game at 1!

Why are almost all of your paragraphs the same size? Anyway —
this is too long for me to read right now. I started it and didn't
really get hooked by the graduation cap and then there may have
been wonderful moments in the story toward the end but I'd've
preferred if you were the one who excavated them, polished them
off, then sent them in. I ain't no literary archeologist, and it seems
this story is like an ancient city covered in dirt — so as Jay-Z says,
go on brush your shoulder off, by which I mean, clarify, purify,
clean, cut, condense, make pretty for tourists.

You say you won't bother with credits and bios but then you go on and on and on about this and that and how you won't bother till every word you write in the introductory note or cover letter or whatever colors the text one way or another and so we humbly advise you to be wary that that's what goes on on this side of the screen and we also proudly say that none of the aforementioned in any way influenced our reading of this submission, which we sort of liked, especially the beginning, but then once there's the frottage session on the train we stopped believing in it and although the writing is clear we had to sort of push our eyes on to the end that was in sight and so all we can say about this is that maybe if you integrated the first part into the second part and deleted all the paragraph breaks or many of them (we don't love that unnecessary formal cliché of online writing) then maybe the feeling that there are two stories here or there's backstory and then story or there are character intros and then story would just seem more like one story without the clear disconnect between the two parts. Whew. We apologize for the use of the royal we above and I apologize for everything and thank you for submitting and wish you luck with this and everything else forever after in the known universe and the next.

People shit on your head for good reason. Lists like this were funny on Letterman in 1986, but back then, they were funny lists. This is not funny. Please rewrite so each thing makes no sense at all and then resend it. You're trying to make sense. You're talking about cats. Talk about monkeys. And crack cocaine. Or talk about some rare breed of snake. You see, maybe something more like: "#5 — Will stop rescuing stray baby sidewinder snakes from supermarket salad bar." Etc. Not that that's funny. But you understand. Ok? Sorry. Have fun. Relax. Smoke 'em if you got 'em. Love your neighbor. Live to send again.

When I see something involving the third grade, my eyes glaze over — I swear it! It's not your fault, nor mine — but my damned eyes! Send another one!

How can you call something Run Rabbit Run like the Updike book without the punctuation?! Also, I suggest you never use the word maudlin again. I also saw it in the thing you sent yesterday. Also, this is too crazy to post. I like the language's instinct but it's too all-over-the-place punny to concentrate on, to care to follow. It's not something to read but to look at. Maybe try refining it a bit and using the rangy language (I like) to serve a clear story? Otherwise, I've just moved to Iowa City where Marilynne Robinson and colleague friends will learn me how to write good creative fiction for at least two years. What's been happening here so far: the cats have been hunting down bunnies the last few days. The thing we've learned is that bunnies make noises, a crazy distress signal, like five high "ehnt-ehnt-ehnt-ehnt-ehnt" blasts and then are silent and all nose sniffling. Who knew? Turns out rabbits aren't on those circular animal noise maker things kids have for good reason! Cow goes moo moo, lamb goes bah bah, bird goes tweet tweet, bunny goes crazy fucking murderous high-alert alarm freakout.

Sorry for the slow reply — this submission got trapped on my computer when I moved recently and I had trouble getting the old girl active. But thanks for submitting — I don't think this is right for Eyeshot — it's perfectly fine but I think you'll have better luck at other sites — it was maybe a bit too formally traditional for this particular site, to be a little more exact. I hate when places reject my shit and say "this wasn't right — good luck" and I realize that's exactly what I'm saying to you but at least I'm throwing down a lot of words around it to show you I care. The truth is I'm an excruciatingly slow typist — the word "excruciatingly" just took me 45 seconds to type, not nearly as long the second time because I copied/pasted the first instance — in fact, I am an exceedingly fast copier/paster—most of the words in this message were actually copied and pasted from other messages — it's just faster for me. I have arthritis and wear very heavy rings on my fingers for some stupid reason pertaining to avant-garde finger style. The rings are so heavy they also keep me from playing guitar, unless I play the guitar like a percussion instrument. Not playing guitar keeps me from remembering that I once thought I'd grow up to be Hendrix. Not like Hendrix as a guitarist. Instead I'd grow up to be Hendrix exactly. Once I hit adolescence I'd begin to look more and more like him every day and act like him and play like him until I was Hendrix. Anyway. Good luck in Croatia. Have you read Danilo Kis?

Eyeshot's Garden, Ashes

Thanks for sending these — I was able to read them all the way through and thought they read cleanly and interestingly. For Eyeshot, I don't think they're quite right. They're very, very, very close though. If I didn't have a ton of contributions ready to go right now I would have accepted these. But having the luxury of being picky and therefore only accepting things that really wow me, I think I'll say thanks and sorry — I'm 100% sure you'll get these posted or published somewhere eventually but I felt there was something too controlled and precise for Eyeshot. Didn't have quite enough air and space and pace and propulsion and improvisation to it. And after reading them, they disappear a little. I mean, I can't quite remember them right now. A ghost-head tortoise? But then again I'm sick and I may have overdosed on NyQuil last night! Anyway, again, despite what the last few lines say, I did like these and will gladly let you know that they're more interesting than most stuff I receive, and that half the time when people send stuff like this that's way more poorly done, I try to direct them so they'll hopefully wind up doing something like what you sent. But I think I would have liked a little more vitality, looseness, vividness, for Eyeshot at least. So thanks again and sorry and good luck. Send more soon.

Thanks for sending something again! I tend not to post things like what you sent — the two involving children I've posted (out of a few hundred received) are sort of strange. One involves dead clowns, the other wooly mammoths. Meaning they're sort of odd. The one you sent is well done and easy to get through and should be able to find a home somewhere, but I try to post things that might not find a home so easily.

It's like the drunk intellectual girl under a cloud of smoke on the bed in Kenzaburō Ōe's *A Personal Matter*, but blond, and way American, and a little extra fleshy, and smoking candy cigs, and not nearly naked enough. Thanks and sorry and good luck.

You write well and you're obviously interested in what you're doing and you take it seriously, so I think I'd suggest for this piece that you take the reader's attention seriously. I really like discursive stuff, but this didn't seem to have the necessary oomph to pull it off. It was like it all led to the revelation of the dream and once you got there, the dream didn't seem emphatically worth the wait. Sorry. But thanks for submitting and I hope you send something that's shorter with more explicit story.

Read Matt Klam's *Sam the Cat* — he does the same sort of thing you do, sort of, but in a way that seems a bit more artful and thereby lessens the blow of the ass talk. But thanks for submitting and good luck.

We don't do dental or, if you check out the archive you'll see we don't do dialogue that much either... thanks for sending it and good luck.

Just because you have Word on your computer doesn't mean you can just type something on a file and send it out. Not to sound like a condescending a-hole, but it doesn't really seem like much effort has been expended or much pressure exerted on the language or much thought put into trying to affect a reader you've never met. So. Thanks and sorry and good luck.

I'm sorry to take so long and even more sorry to pass on this without much explanation — sorry, sorry, sorry — just that I've totally slacked on reading submissions for a while due to sickness after healthy involvement in the world for a while and now I'm looking at many, many submissions and really just looking for ones that totally assert themselves and say accept me, my friend, or maybe even something more brash. I think what happened here with the beginning of your story is that I stopped, thinking about Mike, about naming characters "Mike" instead of Spalding or Sterling or President Bush. And then "gay-appareled" stopped me. Made me wonder about Xmas. Gay elves? David Sedaris? And then I skimmed down and read intermittently and then hit reply and started typing, and before I finished typing I also suggested that maybe you should stick to the "left justify" mode, which doesn't make all those weird varied spaces between words. But thanks again for sending this and sorry for my quick response and not-so-careful consideration — it's really like what I do is scan the language and if it's a match for the site I read much more carefully and if it's not really a match... anyway — thanks again — and best of luck getting this one posted somewhere!

Thanks for sending something again after all these years while we were in a semi-sleeping website silence while at the Midwestern graduate school. We've relocated Eyeshot operations to a $495/month bright/airy tiny apartmento in South Philadelphia where we hesitantly recommence our e-literary online proceedings as though everything in Iowa never happened. I really like the attention you give to the old-timey language — was amazed at how consistently you found the right faux-French adjectives — but for the site I'd like for this to be a bit more explicitly profane and paced a bit quicker? Thanks for sending something again and definitely try with other things whenever.

This one won't really work for ye olde Eyeshot — it's clear, definitely, but it's about domestic relations related to onions, and while that is perfectly understandable and laudable as a launching point for what might have been an unpredictable exploration of stenches, this one wallowed in Vidaliaville for me and didn't really seem to take readers anywhere, right? Think about the person on the other side of the screen — not me — but those so-called "readers. How do you want them to respond to your stuff? How do you want to move and manipulate them, make their minds go mmm? I'm saying I think the issue here is not in the execution but the instinct. I suggest you challenge your conception of what you think a story should be, or more so, what it should DO to a reader?

I think the thing is to compare what you write to things you like to read. If you do that, really do it side by side, you'll see a serious difference between what you sent and what's expected, even in A.M. Homes or Carver or Lipsyte, things considered spare. Good luck — keep at it — all that.

My question for you, I guess, would be why bother? What's the point? Is orgasming in someone's mouth enough? What else is there to this? Could there be more? Can the simple little sensationalist thing of the word orgasm suffice to make anyone wanna post this or read it and then walk away thinking what? The world is not a very beautiful place. Well, the natural world is beautiful but I mean the world we've made isn't always so hot, lots of sorrow and ugliness and self-induced disease and evil ideation, so maybe it's one's duty not to add to all that crap, to make things more beautiful, and by "beautiful" I think I mean elegantly complicated, ecstatic, open, elusive, varied, alive but also caught in amber...

There should probably be more scene, with description integrated into it. Your description is fine, but there's too much too early and the girl you're describing isn't moving — she's just being drawn but not really coming to life, got me? And then you only hint at scenes that don't really exist in particular/described worlds? So I had trouble seeing it. It felt real, though, which is great. But I think you might want to consider trying to up the narrative oomph, tell a story, make the characters come alive as they move through physical space, try to hypnotize the reader with aerodynamic language so the reader can see and feel things that don't exist, that is, imagine stuff. Yeah? You asked if I look for a certain type of story. Not really. I sort of scan the story's literary DNA and then either engage it or skim it. I'm really good at doing that after years of this. I tend to accept things that I read all the way through, that get my attention (in a semi-tasteful, interesting way) and drag me through the story till the end. If my mind wanders after the seventh sentence, all is lost. Hope that helps.

Hi — thanks for the kind words — I read missed connections on craigslist all the time and this could be posted there maybe — I don't think I'm gonna post it though, but thanks for sending it and good luck.

When I taught creative writing I had a rule that kids couldn't write about sex, drugs, rock and roll, murder, perversion, or death. I said this because if I didn't everyone would write about drugs and drink and death. There's everything else to write about! (For example: a plate glass window in love with an ice storm.) I think you write relatively well about drugs and friendship and all, but also maybe stylistically what I was sensing was that I couldn't really sense these kids, and that's what's really important — also the language seemed totally anonymous, which serves you well but isn't exactly what I'm looking for? Anyway — thanks for sending this and good luck with it and send something else whenever.

Thanks for sending this and sorry for the slowish reply. I've been reading too many submissions today and have rejected every one, in part from spite, since I should be outside enjoying the Saturday but am instead inside, a wee bit hungover from spending too much time immersed in smoky karaoke madness at Ray's Happy Birthday Bar, milking the last moments of my youth best I can, and now, unable to do much else, getting submissions out of the way. I enjoyed reading what you sent. I've spent the last few hours reading things that didn't feel real at all, stories with characters named "Mike" who go to the dentist, and it was refreshing to read this and it feels absolutely real, believable, which is what Twain said differentiated fiction from non-fiction (something like "the difference between fiction and non-fiction is that fiction must be absolutely believable"), and while what you sent is almost surely non-fiction, it's also fiction, which is fact arranged in an artful way. Again, I like what you sent and would like to read something else if you'd ever like to send it. I don't think I'm going to post what you sent this time because it's enjoyable and authentic and yet maybe a bit too offhanded or like excerpts from an online travel journal? It definitely activated my voyeuristic capacities but maybe there could be more to it, or maybe it feels a little too easy to forget a second after the pleasurable experience? Anyway — thanks for sending this and sorry and send more?!

The photo you sent of your sister smoking a cigarette is totally smokin'. Your story's first paragraph is good, and so is your language, the rhythm, the aerodynamics. After the first paragraph or so, this one needs to take off, to keep moving. Think of a rocket going into space: this one takes off and then floats instead of intermittently being boosted by a blast of unexpected awesomeness. I thought I'd accept this after the first paragraph, and this thought came after rejecting a few dozen in a row that really have my writerly spirit sinking, and so I was psyched at first but then feel like you can put more effort into this one or can send me something else now or later or whenever, but in general I like your sister, thanks for sending the picture, though maybe she's got an unfortunate nostril issue, and I like your prose, its urgency, its reality, I guess. So send more stuff!

Hematite? I had to look that word up. Thanks for sending this. It's clear but maybe too spare for what I tend to like to post. Have you ever read *A Sport and a Pastime*? Damn that's some fine erotic writing, once you get beyond page 75 or so. Thanks for sending this and sorry and send more whenever, maybe a bit shorter?

YOU ARE SO ENTHUSIASTICALLY ALL OVER THE PLACE! WHICH IS A GOOD THING! WE LIKE ENTHUSIASM AND ENERGY! I WOULD SURELY LIKE TO DRINK ESPRESSO WITH YOU AND RUN AROUND AND CHAT AND THEN HAVE ACROBATIC SPORT SEX. BUT WHEN IT COMES TO READING WHAT YOU'VE WRITTEN IT'S LIKE TOO MUCH Y'KNOW LIKE TOO MUCH ENERGY AND ALL OVER THE PLACENESS AND SPORT SEX WHEN WHAT WE THINK WE REALLY LIKE TO SEE IS MORE CONTROLLED ENERGY NOT MANIA BUT SOMETHING MORE LIKE DIRECTED FOCUSED EFFUSIONS OF FORWARDLY PROPELLED PROSE IF YOU KNOW WHAT I MEAN AND MAYBE SOME LIGHT PETTING AND SLOW CARESSES UNDER A WARM COMFORTER ON A COOL EARLY AUTUMN RAINY MORNING IF YOU KNOW WHAT I'M TALKING ABOUT.

There's something about your language that seems really young, an innocence to it. What you sent isn't really a story. It's a handful of sentences sort of about a dog, like you maybe read some Lydia Davis and then saw a dog and started writing? Maybe I'd suggest to really only bother writing something that seems necessary to write, not to screw around with anything other than what must be written, and also while writing keep in mind that you're trying to affect someone you've never seen, either make them laugh or agitated or randy or sad? There's an innocent manneredness to what you sent that seems like a barrier between you and writing something good, or enjoying and gaining anything from the whole process of writing maybe? Write because you have something to say, is what I'm saying, and try to make it affect another person. But thanks for sending this and hope all's well!

Nice breast pic! But in the third sentence: "Sometimes he'd be stood there"... That ain't right! But thanks for the titty shot. And good luck!

Thanks for sending this but I gots to say sorry man 'cause this is maybe like a little too quick or spare or ADD or something in a way that distracted me. I guess I like to see things that hypnotize me into reading, that assert an authority and an execution of language and propel it all with narrative oomph? But thanks again for sending it and sorry and good luck with it.

Thanks for sending this and sorry for taking a month to look at it! We suck. I suck. You don't suck, but I'm gonna pass on this story because we don't do dental. Good luck getting it posted somewhere and thanks again for considering Eyeshot.

Thanks for sending something and sorry for letting the weekend pass without responding. There's a lot to like in this story, especially the parts that feel real like the taxi ride or the repeated scenes that don't really go anywhere, as scenes in real life so often fizzle, so there's a mimetic thing I like about this throughout, but at the same time I'm not so sure if it really goes anywhere in a satisfying way for this reader, which might intentionally be the case, but if so maybe the language could come up a notch or two, otherwise what's the pleasure in reading the existential unease of the sensitive urban male — similar stories I've written, autobiographical maybe to a fault, maybe too filled with reflections of life more than an organization and deployment of that life into something more meaningful than real life, a.k.a. "art"? Thomas Wolfe says that fiction is fact selected, arranged, and charged with purpose, and I think this story doesn't quite feel propelled or charged with a purpose other than depicting unsatisfactory encounters, rather consistently and often well. I kept looking for an alternative starting point, since there was something I liked about it and thought I might be able to post an excerpt, but each scene, self-consciously I think, edged away from intrigue or development, a series of episodes that stream together, segued with moments where the dude is alone, thinking... So. With all that said, I'm psyched you sent this and hope you send other stuff in the future, maybe shorter and more committed either to performative language spiels or a flowing, engaging narrative? Or something else. Say hi to the old neighborhood for me. (I'm always on the verge of moving back there.) And check out Beat the Devil at Union Pool on Friday — they feature a hot diminutive Indian-American lady who plays harmonium and reminds me of Morrison or Iggy Pop or Nick Cave.

REJECTION LETTERS FROM THE EYESHOT OUTBOX

The bit about the vibrator enjoying cave exploration is pretty clever but this is maybe just a bit too senselessly mildly amusingly graphic. I'm just not sure who would appreciate it or find it funny, so I'll thank you and pass on it.

My first impression was that the guy's name can't be Carver, or it could be but then you'd need to change the prostitute's name to Paley or Lessing or Sontag. The larger issue related to that name I think is that it never feels real, always feels like a story to me, which is fine if it then feels more like a fable, like a tale, but this feels like a story that has some wonderful moments, sharp evocative lines, like when it's mentioned that he was thankful for all the TV he'd watched, implying that the conversation was nostalgic and not so heady, but I guess it doesn't quite feel like it's something I can really SEE, because what I was seeing the whole time was the writing, the story's story-ness, and the goal I guess is to get the reader to see past the language while simultaneously admiring it. Hmm. Anyway. Thanks a lot for sending this. I'm definitely going to post things more frequently, considering I have some more time and would like to have an active Eyeshot back out in the world. Thanks again and sorry and send some more stuff whenever.

My first impression is that this is a little long and a little overwritten — though I admire and support highly detailed writing, it's a tightrope — how do you write with imagery and abstractions and piled-up modifiers without stalling a sentence's essential aerodynamics? The thing to do I think is to be really careful of certain words like espied and tumescent and others that sound highfalutin or stodgy — if you purposefully overwrite, the key I think is to choose high and low words and make sure that your primero stylistic concern is forward propulsion. And that brings in the whole thing about content, since you also want to be able to see through the words to what they signify, right? So. Anyway — thanks again for submitting and sorry and hope you get this posted or published elsewhere.

I like the way you write. The first part of this is mainly presentation-of-consciousness stuff and then the second part is dramatized. At first I thought that maybe the first part didn't have quite enough glue to it, meaning my eyes weren't sticking maybe because there were some semi-whimsical moments with hermit crabs and filet mignon innuendo and sexing up mermaids. I thought maybe the beginning could be shortened or streamlined for posting online? And then the story continued and totally shifted from an engaging if not quite totally sticky representation of consciousness to dialogue that I wasn't interested in reading, so I skimmed to the end. The language is attentive and errorless and all, but I guess, right now reading this, I wasn't all that into the situation or the world those words expressed? Anyway. Thanks for sending something and good luck finding a home for it. The sensibility (mermaid sex, waiting on the beach for a raft, etc) matches Eyeshot's historical tendencies, but maybe next time send something a little shorter and maybe a bit more balanced in terms of consciousness and dramatization? Or not. Thanks again and sorry.

I really liked when the lights went off and the cherry of the cigarette could be seen better. I think the whole thing might need to be like that, actually — intensely focused images! Otherwise, well, it's a story about a boy jacking off looking at some girl-next-door love forlorn, and while the language is serviceable it seems maybe not totally honed enough to pull this off, that is, to keep the "so what?" question from entering the reader's brain and getting all tangled up in evoked images. What else? I like the general instinct but maybe less so the ambition and oomph and so I think I'll pass on it and thank you for sending something and ask you to send something again some time and I'll also wish you well in a final sentence of considerable length and thank you again and apologize for the same-day service of this potentially annoying, earnest response. Happy new year and remember it will soon be springtime.

Not sure what to say about the story. I liked the bit about taking sleeping pills to sleep in the sack with Grace. I was a little worried about the semi-demented repetition of her name to begin many sentences, when after the title I was pretty sure that the pronoun "she," if repeatedly used, might refer to this lady. A few typos, including one at the end of the first paragraph. Reminded me at times of some of Tao Lin's simplicities, but then words like televisually etc sort of undercut that. The return of the "poignant" tomato sauce thing at the end, hmm. So. Yeah. I guess I must thank you once again and apologize and thank you and apologize and hope that the swiftness of the response overcomes any annoyance. I'm an oft-rejected writer and I absolutely freakin' abhor the form-letter received after six months. Good luck with everything and say hello to something special in Cambridge for me, like the falafel at the Middle East?

Way too fucking short, my friend. Please browse our archive.

Thanks for deciding to start writing and also thanks for sending this to Eyeshot. It's pretty smooth and sort of funny and definitely makes sense. I laughed about shirtless Iggy entering Starbucks and Mom's Moody Blues remark. Overall, I liked it, thought it had a good instinct and friendly tone, but I guess maybe I also thought there could have been a little more than mentioning a rock-related coincidence at a Starbucks to someone twenty years younger. Your language is enjoyable and clean but maybe you could crank the ambition engines a bit higher next time — or maybe all my suggestions swerve toward fictional revamping anyway — or maybe, even for a non-fictional piece, it'd be cool to get away from Iggy and focus more on the slow/soft trauma of aging, of losing possession of the stuff that had once been so totally yours, that soundtracked life, etc. Or maybe not. Again, I liked this okay but maybe would have appreciated some more oomph? Maybe try *Barrelhouse*? (I always refer Eyeshot's pop-related rejects to them.) Good luck and thanks again for sending something and happy New Year.

I guess the first thing I can say is that it's too long for what I'd like to post now, and the second thing is that no matter the length I might not be all that psyched to post language like "He looked at the girl's breasts again. They were big and soft." I don't know what to do with that. I agree with the old adage that writing, somewhat, is about making the familiar seem miraculous and the miraculous seem familiar. I'm not quite sure what this story is doing, with this dude named "Hell." He doesn't feel real. And yet he doesn't feel totally unreal, either. It's like he's caught in this unreal reality that is right now comprised of what might be called "the stuff of story world." Granted, I didn't read all 17 pages, but the tone, the atmosphere, the sense of the language, that is, the things I really look for, seem underdone while maybe the characters and the story and its world are not quite focused and made material just yet? Anyway. Thanks for sending something. I appreciate it. And hope this quick and honest response is somewhat helpful, even if you totally disagree. It'll at least give you something to think about. Keep at it. Sounds like ridiculous/lame advice, but it's really all that matters. Sitting thy ass down and making more of this stuff till you create real unrealities or something like that. Good luck.

I like what you sent okay — I like the repetition and the self-awareness and the writing colony stuff — it seems like a sort of exercise, maybe, sort of self-consciously so — I don't think I'll post it because maybe I'd like to post some things in this new late-to-mid-decade era that are maybe clearer and more flowing and entertaining, less elusive. It's real well written, except for a minor typo midway, but I guess I'd like to post some things with maybe a bit more oomph? Anyway. Send more stuff whenever. And thanks again.

Thanks for sending this story and pic. I tend to post most of the pics, so forget about that. The story, I think I can say a few quick and hopefully helpful things about: the first would be the second person thing, which immediately distances things for this reader at least. The second tense tends to be best for describing really traumatic events, I think, because then the distancing seems more like a psychological plausible tactic than simply a fictionalizing technique, like this is basically about "I," but if you say "you," it'll feel more fictional and less like a diary or blog. The second thing has to do with your instinct at this point, I think. And I write the following having written things like this when I was younger: of course it might be "total fiction" carefully crafted to seem like non-fiction, but still. I think you might want to always keep in mind why a reader who has possibly at one time before been 23 years old and out of college and facing life and maybe has some distance on such an era might want to read this presentation of the same thing, especially when the actions or details here are sort of defused over time. For a story like this to engage me, I think it'd need to be more focused in time, a pivotal moment, not a sort of continual recent past involving semi-blandish occurrences. I might have missed something exciting or engaging or peculiar, but I only did so because I skimmed after a while. Why? Because it's not focused in time and therefore there's more pressure for the prose to entertain or hold the reader's attention, and while the prose is fine, it's not tense enough or interesting enough really to activate this reader's interest in the situation, which isn't really much of a concentrated or dramatic one, right? So. With all that said, I'd maybe just think about considering the reader more and focusing things. Make a world come alive though precise sensory description. Make some people, other than some shadow self, come alive. But mainly always ask yourself how this story might possibly interest a psychologically and emotionally (semi-) mature reader. That's all for now. Good luck with everything.

This is like the sixth submission I've read in three days that has involved the dentist. Something is very wrong with the world if the world's writers think that writing about the dentist is gonna turn readers on. There's an entire world out there, and yet writers write about the dentist office, as though there is no other event worth writing about than a dentist visit. I need to update the submission guidelines posthaste! Never again send dentist stories! Otherwise, you write clearly but I think you might want to think about syntax, like maybe you're starting sentences too often with "When," which creates a predictable feeling in readers that can be undermined in fun ways like a joke setup, but otherwise if the second clause ain't unpredictable, eyes glaze. Thanks again for the kind words and thanks for sending this — I hope you get it posted somewhere and I hope you one day try Eyeshot again with something about going to visit the Hunger Artist.

Thanks for sending this. I don't much make distinctions between fiction and non-fiction. I loved this line: "And like one of those young male wolf spiders who sears the leg-band markings of the first female he ever sees into his memory and then forever seeks it out in his mates, I will always expect to find a stash of prohibition-era port secreted in my wainscoting." I pretty much accepted this at that point, but then, very sadly, I couldn't really get into the rest. You're trying to write a little too hard, I think. As a reader, I can sense that insignificant sentences have been over-considered. So maybe I'd suggest writing faster and try to keep in mind that the reader does not care what you care about. For example, I had trouble caring about this story, the situation. I really like the notion of hidden rooms, but sneering at the $2 tip and the Marge Simpson reference didn't quite engage me — that's the main thing: I think this might benefit if the sense of it were somehow more urgent than precious? And by "precious" I mean over-considered or literary or, at the end with the return of the hidden rooms thing, essayistic. Hmm. I don't know! Send more?!

If this didn't involve big cats it wouldn't be all that interesting, and the inclusion of big cats doesn't really push it too far toward interesting, actually, I think. Sorry. My only advice would be to not think that the inclusion of an oddity is all the work that needs to be done. But thanks again for sending it and sorry.

My advice is to take two months off from writing to read the Briggs translation of *War and Peace* — thanks for sending this, though.

Someone needs to tell you that this sort of writing is not so hot. Someone needs to tell you that you need to read better lit and then emulate it and then gradually discover your own style. Someone needs to tell you that what you sent has no basis in anything that's been published before, but still this sort of stuff is not original. At best, if I were to post it, it would perpetuate the idea that the web is a repository for amateurish work. It's readable and maybe similar to what clever undergrads write who haven't read nearly enough and don't have a knowledge of or respect for any sort of literary tradition. Most editors wait three months before sending a form rejection. I send a next-day challenge to humble yourself, read a lot, and raise your game. Read at least thirty pages a day of good lit. If you need recommendations, I've got some. You write very clearly and your stuff is readable — major advantages — but that's only the first rung up a never-ending ladder of complexities. Keep at it and read, read, read, read, read. Then look at what you sent again.

You write very cleanly but I'm not sure what you write about, or more so, I'm not sure too many people might come away from reading this feeling like they've been infected with some new perception, a sharpened sense of the world, or even just feeling that their love for lit has been temporarily requited. People love reading, the love is out there, it's waiting for you, you just got to give readers something loveable to love! Something that stirs them. That differentiates itself among unlovable minions. Readerly love is unlike motherly love. It's absolutely conditional. Don't expect readers protected behind computer screens won't sneer, roll eyes, get bored. The idea is to hypnotize them, woo them. I'd suggest you put more pressure on your language and characters and dialogue and read 20+ top contemporary and canonical books before 2008 is up. Thanks for submitting and good luck.

There's too much significance seemingly embedded in every sentence. Every sentence feels "weighty" because of the syntax. But when you look into each sentence and read the whole thing, it's more a sensation than something with real heft. Which is another way of saying that, formally, this feels false to me (i.e., fictional — but your syntax, your "fictional" approach, for me, undermines believability, I think). Second, the second person distracts me unless it's used to deal with major, massive events or some scenario that's absolutely unfamiliar. Otherwise, it makes me want to reread Lorrie Moore. Third, despite the fish symbolism (men, messiah), the story is weighed down by what a teacher of mine (see "Letters to Frank Conroy From His Students" on Eyeshot) called "abject naturalism," that is, the over-description of every movement. This sort of thing so often manifests in kitchen scenes, and it kills readerly interest. So: that seems to be enough — it feels false formally and it's overly symbolic in terms of content. It reads cleanly, though, which is certainly a plus. But I think something you might want to think about is love. Readers want to love. They have this great storehouse of love waiting to be requited. So try to give them something to love! But what's that mean? Meet them halfway, entertain, enlighten, enliven brains, stir hearts, stab guts, fondle loins, make 'em run, and finally let 'em stand tall and think they've seen something in their imagination that's cast a real shadow.

It's a little longer than what I tend to post, but I liked how it started and you dropped some serious names in the bio note and maybe it's time to start posting longer stories? This one's footer says it's for the Zoetrope All-Story contest. My guess is you didn't win, huh? Sorry. It's a very clearly written story, reliant on exposition, and the narration is intelligent and insightful, but about 1/3rd of the way through, for me, the narrative tone/tack got a bit burdensome, and then it kept going on like that. It opens with a suggestion of a scene, but then goes into the character's lineage and description, for example. I guess it seems like, for a story so reliant on exposition, that the dramatic situation, the story's "engine," could be revved up some more, started earlier in a way that energizes the reader to cruise through all the backstory about mama? The problem, for me, was that after about 1/3rd of the way through, my attention was wandering a little, so when I got to the part about White's grave and then got more exposition about him, I wanted to come up for air in a dramatized present? By which I mean I was swamped and maybe didn't catch everything in the story after that bit or make all the connections by the end, largely because I was bored, ultimately, so why bother going back to reread? That's about as honest a response I can give you for why I'm passing on the story you kindly submitted to my pissant website. You really write well, but I think maybe you might want to consider another draft or two on this one? Also, maybe consider occasionally varying the syntax, or more so, the sentence length. After a while it seemed like every sentence measured exactly the same distance, and that gets a little hypnotic/soporific sometimes. Anyway, thanks and definitely send something again soon, maybe something a little shorter? Or longer if it rocks.

Hi — thanks for sending something again — I like this one much better — it feels much more real, almost more like a personal essay than a story, and I like that. But I guess there's also something I'm looking for in the language, a formal sort of pressure on the text, that I don't quite sense here. Not that it needs to have that sort of pressure, because it's about a young kid, but maybe the language could offer more sensations for the reader, more touches and tastes, images that make the world come more to life — more "showing," as they say, even if the story summarizes most of what could otherwise, in a much longer story, be presented as scenes with dialogue and all. Anyway, thanks for sending this and keep at it. Read as much as you can of all that good stuff in old-fashioned print books and keep pushing yourself and send again whenever. Good luck.

The meta stuff, to me, sends up unnecessary interference. Meta stuff was maybe sort of cool thirty years ago, but *Scream* and *Another Teen Movie* killed it dead. If you use meta-tactics, you got to figure out some clever new way to pull it off, not just ape it and think it inherently cool. It's inherently distracting and annoying, actually — the challenge is to make it work really well thematically. Check out the first story in Nam Le's *The Boat*, which just came out — "Love and Honor and Pity and Pride and Compassion and Sacrifice" is a great meta story about writing ethnic fiction, a story in which I have a fictionalized cameo as a drunk lunatic ranting about Faulkner's old verities (if you read it, you'll see that the narrator gets shot in the leg with an air-rifle pellet, but in reality, I did — such is the art of fiction!). But the way you've used the meta thing, it just confounds any clear image for a reader, I think. Maybe check out *War and Peace* and then think about what tack you'd like to take as a writer afterwards? Anyway, I respect the experiment though and think you have a pretty solid sense of rhythm, so don't hate me. Thanks for submitting and sorry and send more whenever you feel like it.

That's really kind of you to think that I might want to post your novel on my pissant website! I know how long it takes to make those freakin' things, and so I totally respect whatever path led you to think Eyeshot would be a reasonable hosting spot. With that said, I can't really say that I've read your book. It's way too long, and I'm reading Houellebecq's *Platform* right now and working on my own extended stuff and essays and whatnot. I read some of the opening and thought it readable and relatively righteous, but then skimmed down and saw a lot of screenplay-style stuff that scared me. More so: I'd say don't give up working on it. I'm sorry that I just don't really have the time to read it properly and post it or make helpful suggestions, but most short submissions I can really pretty much decide on in a matter of seconds, and doing so with a novel would be unfair. A good title, maybe a good book? You owe it to the work you did on it, not to mention your teacher Tom Grimes, to try to find it a more reasonable home than the good olde irrational Eyeshot. Thanks for sending it though and good luck and let me know when it sees the light of day.

It's almost like one of those prose poems that people received for a while as spam e-mail. I like its instinct and attitude! But I think it's too much to process, too much effort (for me at least) with reward mainly in an appreciation of the phrasing, but I can't really stick with it enough to excavate theme? Anyway. Send more, send shorter? What are you thinking about when you're doing this sort of stuff?

I like your instinct a lot. Descriptive and sensory, almost paranormally aware of things, overly sensitive like a Ouija board with the fingertips of the world pressing lightly on you? I've lived in Boston (a while in Brighton on Commonwealth but mainly in JP on Rockview) and currently live in South Philly over by Pat's and Geno's. So I could see the places you're writing about, but also what you've written reminds me of some of the things I wrote when I lived in Boston and was alone a lot 12 years ago. I know what Storrow Drive looks like, what 11th and South (there's a CVS) looks like in Philadelphia, but most other readers don't. Not sure how much that matters compared to the mental state, which comes through the prose pretty well — a little over-romantic maybe but not flowery, a little prone to melancholy, desirous, attentive, going for it but not exactly always hitting things right on? Hmm. I like what you sent but won't post it but I will ask you to send more whenever! Something to maybe think about is that this sort of thing sometimes comes off as a bit too personal, meaning that the reader can't necessarily see and sense all the things the writer sees and senses, so the writer needs to be a bit more generous sometimes in terms of description and orientation, present a little bit cleaner surface maybe. By "cleaner," I mean occasionally varying the depth at which things are happening in the narrator's head? Anyway — thanks again for sending it and send more!

I'm not sure I like this one as much as the first one. I think you're doing a sort of automatic writing, highly alliterative, that you could condense and conform toward conventionality in terms of telling a story to please a reader? Anyway — I like the instinct but it's like an impenetrable language thicket. I'd prefer more penetration. (That sounds nasty, I realize.)

I write extremely short rejection letters: no.

Eyeshot tends not to post dialogue-heavy pieces, but the good news is that tons of sites welcome dialogue-heavy stories, but not nearly as many prefer balls-to-wall exposition, as we like to call it. We are the home of the brave, that is, in terms of balls-to-wall exposition, and the land of the free, that is, in terms of balls-to-wall exposition. I've never described Eyeshot as the home or the land of anything, especially not balls-to-wall exposition. This is the first time I've used that phrase to describe the sort of balls-to-wall exposition we prefer to post. Why do we do that? Because we prefer it, simple as that. I realize this isn't approaching thematic feedback re: your submission, but, re-reading it now, I see there's a lot more than just dialoguey form. It's amusing and inventive and proceeds associatively and insanely, which we like — I particularly like the fourth paragraph. But I think for Eyeshot I'd prefer a little more balls-to-wall exposition, of course! All this I write in order to encourage you to keep at it and read Russell Edson and send more whenever.

Hi—thanks for sending this. Who isn't a big fan of breasts? For the first part of this I was into it. I really liked the bit about raw cabbage, about rubbing garlic on the unfavored nipple. At that point I was thinking I might post this, but then the yoga instructor thing seemed a little too exaggerated, and then when we meet Bill from South Carolina, I started to lose interest and soon after initiated editorial skimming capacities till I reached the end, whereupon I hit reply and wrote "Hi" etc above. So now we're here. What now? I like the way you write, mainly. It's energetic, if sometimes a little too much so maybe? Maybe all sentences feel as though they consist of between 10 and 25 words? Maybe sometimes drop a fragment in there, or shorter bursts, if just to vary the syntax and keep eyes on the page a little more? I felt like I was riding the energy of each sentence and each sentence was equally energized, which ultimately undid my readerly energy? That sounds hella new-agey, I know. Sorry. Anyway — good luck with everything, and send more whenever.

I started to check out a little bit when the word "mien" showed up and then never really reached a point where I was engaged or cared for these people or the way they're expressed in prose. I don't think you're putting enough pressure on the language or the story. It all feels like a chunk of coal, unsaturated with lighter fluid, untouched by fire. Squeeze that shit tight with maximum imaginative/editorial pressure till it's a bright-burning diamond.

Thanks for sending something again, so promptly — determination should always be respected and rewarded with semi-prompt, in-depth responses. I guess my semi-prompt, in-depth response is the same as the last one I sent. You seem really admirably aware of your language, but I honestly think it's overdone and not as generous in terms of creating images in the reader's mind (this mind, at least) as you might hope? For example: "hope gulped whole" is a pretty sweet phrase, but it comes after "caressing with teeth like fangs and her mouth drips with agony's soft splashes," which to my Pro-Overindulgence eye and ear seems like way too much—more so, it's over-the-top but not self-aware of its over-the-topness or using its over-the-top energy to get at something outside itself ("Any book worth its salt points up and out of itself"— Bohumil Hrabal). I guess that's the thing, the difference, the rub in our sensibilities? I love overindulgent, over-the-top, essentially overwritten language (Mark Leyner always, DFW often, Philip Roth sometimes, Nabokov/Updike to a degree) but only when it's having more self-aware, flight-of-fancy fun? And maybe I like when it serves a character or a clear idea, more so — when it's channeled in a more discernible direction? This seems to serve a character who's maybe way too much inside her head for me to follow and dig in there and come away with the glory? Maybe at first you need to build a bridge to the reader with some easier language, some simple suggestion of situation and setting to orientate folks at the beginning before dropping the rungs off ye olde language ladder? But, again, what you're doing, focusing so much on the language, is admirable as an instinct and as practice, but I think, as part of the execution of that instinct, it just needs to maybe have conciliatory textures that reach out to more rational reader folks on the other side of the aisle. (I'm obviously overloaded with election lingo.) Anyway! Thanks again for submitting this and keep at it and good luck and send again whenever!

Hi — Thanks for sending this. Maybe read Huxley's *The Doors of Perception*? I like a good ol' acid adventure, but this is a little too bouncy to really make me feel the strychnine bite on not the best stuff? Anyway — thanks again for sending it and good luck.

This is sort of textual Halloween, what with the word "guts" appearing, a word I've never allowed on Eyeshot. Sorry.

I think that for what you're doing to be considered "legitimate" by editors, you need to master things like the hyphenation of compound adjectives and also copyedit your stuff till it's totally perfect. For example: "self induce myself into a comma"? That's the first battle, without which you'll never proceed to much more difficult battles, like imprinting an image in a reader's brain, then modulating that image, dragging it from their head to loins to guts to heart. My not-really-professional editorial opinion of your writing is this: you have a wonderfully unpredictable, nonconformist instinct, something that can't really be taught, but you're maybe a bit too confident right now that a reader is going to follow you, is going to keep reading after the fifth sentence about 37 erections, right? I think you need to be more anxious about the appearance of your text and also about losing a reader almost right away. Maybe always picture that, on the other side of the screen, is an impatient person who's read and lived way more than you have. Let a little bit of old-fashioned standard editorial work serve your instinct and thereby improve the language you're apparently sort of maybe a little too easily excreting right now. Essentially, I'm saying there's more to writing than having fun composing—there's also a super-serious aspect to it called "editing" — I'd suggest, as an exercise in disciplining your instinct, try to devote 90% more time to editing than to composing right now — that is, if you give a shit about this. If not, don't bother. If you're half-assed about it, consider whether your time could be better put to use or if you want to devote a little more of your ass to it (meaning: read as much as possible)? Anyway — sorry to rant — just trying to help.

Hi. Thanks for sending this readable short piece involving a bat that comes into the house. That is, a black flapping blur. Dad swings at it with a baseball bat. There's a suggestion that there's some tension between Mom and Dad. Dad swings and misses at the bat in the house with the bat in his hands and then he gets very angry. Despite his anger, the black flapping blur is still in the house, representing familial tension. The bat (not the black flapping blur) shatters and a piece goes into Mom's LEFT eye, not her RIGHT eye, but her sinister eye, the eye on the left side of her body that's ruled by the right side of her brain, that is, the creative side of her, the side that is like a black flapping blur itself, the flexible side, the side that would never wield a baseball bat against a black flapping blur but instead would open the windows wide and let the monster produced by the sleep of reason find its way out.

Hi—thanks for your note and taking the time to submit and caring about trying to get your stuff on the silly little website I've edited for like EXACTLY nine years now. I really think today may be the ninth anniversary that the thing went live in whatever weird form it was in back then, with four of my early/unpublishable-elsewhere stories posted under pseudonyms. Anyway. I like the disguised thing but am not going to post it. It's maybe too deeply embedded in your (the writer's) brain and so the reader (me) has to do a little too much work to dredge out the basic orientating gist? That can be a good thing if done perfectly (see: Grace Paley) but it's tough too. Anyway — keep sending — keep working on stuff for yourself and never tailor your stuff for a shit-ass little website — make it matter to you and to someone else.

Thanks for submitting but I think I'm going to pass on this but not really tell you why. Feel free to reject my rejection, it's really a pretty worthless one. Really, I'm just looking for something to hold my interest — and this one, like the Spurs against Kobe, couldn't contain me.

Norman Mailer wouldn't even bother to squash you like a beetle beneath his boot. There are literary battles, actually, but I guess we're at war or something? Anyway — thanks for sending this — maybe read more than worry about writing about literary battles? Sorry — but thanks again for sending it.

Hey there — good luck with your site — don't give up on it when the wonder wears off and try to respect submissions more than think of them as a chore, that's what editing a lit site or journal or whatever is really all about — receiving submissions and figuring out which ones you'd like to champion/validate and associate yourself with and make a little more accessible — the actual editing and formatting of the pieces is minimal compared to vetting submissions — it seems that so-called editors think their so-called job involves something more than reading submissions, and therein lies the rub with so many venues — editors stall the process through laziness and disrespect writers and undermine the whole process — but since you're a writer, you know what writers want to receive from editors: a quick response and honest (possibly kind, helpful, but never bullshitty) reaction. As far as what you sent, I'm not sure why I would want to champion or validate or associate myself with it (and other things I've posted) or make what you sent more accessible to the world? Jimmy doesn't exist. Who cares about Dennis Leary? "Tapping where the water droplets slither on the panes like ninjas" is a fine image and a model for later work (maybe every sentence can one day be that clear and good?), but the thing about the device and the doctor suggests some malady that's unclear and therefore clouded my attention/engagement — I mean, it starts with checkers and seems to end with some sort of Scrabble, but closer review shows that it's a communication pad affixed to the kid's chest? Maybe you're writing too quickly and not thinking about what someone else cares about when they read a story? The "weight of this one's worth" all rests of an unclear suggestion re: the communication malady (like a serious stutter, I imagine, per your other submissions?), but since it's unclear and ends so quickly, without elaboration, theme/variation, emphasis, there's nothing to champion or validate or associate with or make more accessible — suggestion of a communication malady and related loneliness (solo checkers) isn't enough, I think — there needs to be more to it... Anyway — sorry for unsolicited Polonius-grade ranting re: editing and good luck with the site and the writing and have an optimistic new year!

We are literary fundamentalists when it comes to capitalization. Sorry.

In both stories you sent today, women have well-described pedicured toes. Why? What are these toes about? What does it tell a reader? Why should a reader care about Alisha? Is she African American? Is that an African-American type name? What did she do before? Does she have a husband (someone must have fathered Angel)? Can't she just sell her white Volvo — why WHITE Volvo? Why TAN suit? Why RED toes? What's going on with these colors—or are they arbitrary (that is, simply descriptive)? Are any descriptions simple or do they all characterize and evoke a specific world? Is this story supposed to be commentary on the news, on downsizing, on contemporary economic anxieties? Why should someone read this instead of read the newspaper? What's the role of fiction? Ezra Pound said that literature is "news that stays news"— does your story qualify as "lit" according to this quotation? Meaning: why bother with Alisha? The anxiety of getting a job to pay for prep school is understandable and fine for a story, expressed via the shoes, OK, but what about the formal choices you've made: the way the story is told is very straightforward, not particularly swervy or evocative or embedded in Alisha's particular human psychology? So how might this read if recast as a stream-of-consciousness piece focused on the moment she carries the snakeskin shoes to the interview, with all other elements in the story bubbling up in an organic, associative, nonlinear way, with various anxieties listed in quick sentence fragments, a montage of clips from worst-case scenes? Would that make for a more interesting experience for a reader, esp. in such a short piece? Would doing something like that, reorganizing the approach and situating the story in a single moment that presents the main character's consciousness (i.e., her thoughts/ senses) make Alisha feel like more of a human artfully expressed in carefully composed language than a flat character in a fictional story? My suggestion for now, beyond this story, would be to read as much as you can of good lit and try your best to emulate the stuff you like best. Compare a page of your prose side by side to a page of prose by a writer you really admire: note the difference in syntax, language, characterization, etc.

Hi — thanks for sending something again, Ms. Facebook Friend. I guess my honest reaction is that the short-stuttery syntax got in the way as I read, distracted me from seeing something clearly: a mermaid, a fish, a fishy dream of your typical contemporary American neurotic chick? Maybe if I were to give unsolicited advice re: your approach to writing things like this it'd be to write with way more clear and confident id-fulness than superego, I guess, which seems to get in the way of getting your stroll on? Like I imagine you writing this without words like "cherishloved," for example, and with flowing, compound, sensory-activating sentences. Anyway — thanks for sending this and definitely send something again whenever.

Thanks for sending this lovely, clear-as-clean-undies thong song of a submission. It's maybe just not exactly the sort of thing I'm looking to post. This could almost be an article in a magazine, maybe, but I guess I'm looking for things that would never be considered acceptable opposite an advertisement featuring a nearly naked, very sexually satisfied model trying to sell chocolate-covered mothballs. By which I mean, I just woke up and am not making much sense, but I thank you for sending this, it reads well, it should have no trouble finding a home, just that it maybe makes too much sense for a room at La Casa Eyeshot?

I had a tough time getting into this — I was staring at it for a while and then realized I'd zoned out—why? Maybe because of sentences like this: "Or that we, as a couple, are a desert as a people and so torn that never in the stream of things can we collide, and touch as pieces." Huh? What's that mean? What do I see? What is a "desert as a people"? Can a desert be torn? Can a torn desert people stream along with the stream of WHAT things?! Can a torn streaming desert collide or even touch? Such sentences are launching off points for readerly distraction, the opposite of what writing does when it works well, that is, focuses attention, sharpens it, makes someone imagine something, feel something, that isn't there. If you think of it as a transmission, sentences like this are garbled — if your cable TV showed sentences like this, you'd call them to complain and come check the wires. Seriously! Anyway — thanks for sending this and sorry, but I also think you have a good instinct, just that its execution could be more precise and clear. Anyway — good luck with it.

Hi — thanks for sending this — I like the instinct of the prose, "words rolling over words" as you described it — but maybe with this one I couldn't quite see too deeply beyond the language (a few errors in there distracted too). When you got to Susie, I didn't see this name come to life. Maybe that's my fault. But again I like the instinct, just prefer to SEE a world more than see language, or more so: I prefer to see both simultaneously, like chewing gum and walking. Thanks for sending this and sorry and good luck and send more whenever.

Eyeshot doesn't traffic in subtle realizations. A character realizing something about herself is not the sort of thing I tend to post. Unless she realizes she's something surprising, most likely unhuman, if not necessarily undead.

Thanks for sending this — it's clear and suggests the scene and situation and I like the bit about Cindy Sherman and the last few lines, especially the last one, but I guess it didn't motivate me to type an acceptance letter. I really have little control over the editorial process. There's something else that runs it: I merely do the bidding of the all-powerful capital-R "Response" residing equally in my head, heart, guts, and loins, and somewhat above my head and maybe also in my feet and knees, to a lesser extent. Anyway, this is a perfectly fine thing you've sent but the spirit didn't move me — the Response didn't leap through my fingertips, but send again whenever.

I like the way you write, since we have the same instinct, I think, writing-wise. Energy, sound, sense, flow, pushing ahead clearly to hold the reader's eyes on the words and move things forward ("profluence," they call it). Eyeshot is definitely a home for this sort of writing, but the issue I have with what you sent is the content, particularly the words "mad" and "madness." I think if you took out all psychiatric terms and brand names and changed the title, you might have something here, in that the madness would be on display, wonderfully, but not announced repeatedly. It's like an interesting independent band referring to their music as "indie rock." If you're gonna be "mad" never use the word "mad," since it sort of undermines everything? Anyway — send me something else!

Hi — your bio isn't all that pretentious. I tend to like things like what you sent, recasting a form for some effect. This reads clearly but I guess the deal for me is that I expected that by at least the middle, maybe even earlier, things would start to modulate, get odder, darker, a little more satirical maybe, and certainly at the end reveal the acronym (a must)! The good thing about set forms like infomercials is that they allow for awesome moments when the voiceover busts out of the form, right? Mainly I think that, as this is now, the form overwhelms the effect. Also, I sensed some authorial condescension in the Vietnam Vet's voice with the repetition of "thing's here." Anyway — thanks for sending this and definitely send more stuff whenever.

I think maybe the deal with my response, as clearly as I can say it while sort of sleep deprived (been waking up before 6 am to write for a few hours before heading to work so I can finish a long novel I've been working on since the end of grad school), is that this is autobiographical and fragmentary, or really organically structured and loose (if just to diagnose the submission's gist). None of which is not postable. It's also interesting to read in that it's honest, straight up, not really "crafted" or performative. It's like something you might write for yourself, a diary. As a "story," I think you could maybe think of it as like performing a monologue. If you improvised a monologue and delivered it alone in your bedroom, for someone with a secret eye on it, it'd be interesting and voyeuristic and all, but as a performance, the improvised aspect might make for some moments that lag or lose the interest of the eye in the bedroom sky? And then if the same monologue were performed on a small stage at a bar where people were getting a touch drunk, it's possible that what you sent might not have the authority and oomph to staunch the instinct of a semi-drunken audience to engage in some dialogue whilst you monologue re: the shrink and pah, right? I guess what I'm talking about is crowd control, shepherding attention to your words so everyone in attendance receives your transmission? Again, I like the sense that it's like watching you recall some scenes, and I think the end is well done with dad's last line, so much so that it almost entirely saves the day or like crystallizes everything that came before it, but not really enough for me to post this. Anyway, thanks for sending it and I expect to see more stuff someday.

REJECTION LETTERS FROM THE EYESHOT OUTBOX

This is juvenile. No.

It's well done but maybe I guess I just don't really want to post this because maybe as it reveals all the wreckage it doesn't also offer enough light? It's not so fun to go through these scenes and nothing is really gained from it except relief that when you look away from the screen you're back in your cozy little world. I guess I try to deal more in earthly delights, no matter how freakishly Bosch-like horrific, than the sort of thing you sent. Sorry. But thanks for sending it and good luck.

OK. Fine. I read it again after receiving your explanation. The ending isn't terrible but the whole deal in general is sort of clichéd, right? What's the emotion created in a reader other than a dirty pathetic feeling that makes you want to go brush your teeth immediately. Yeah, OK, it evokes the feeling of a Tuesday night with a drunk husband half-disgusted that he's half-raping his ugly wife. Ugh. Why present such a scene? Also, despite the "realism," it doesn't actually feel real — it feels like a story, a manipulation of the reader. Why drag someone through that? Just so you can draw two semi-unreal people in charcoal beneath the "night's" (as opposed to the "day's") stars, and a nice-sounding phrase about shredded silver that doesn't really even make sense when you try to imagine it? Anyway — maybe you'll get this posted somewhere that's not interested in any sort of "delight," even the horrific kind. Good luck.

Thanks for sending this and sorry for the slow reply — I read it right away when I received it and almost responded then but got distracted at work, and then there was Thanksgiving, a holiday during which I am not allowed to read submissions or else be stricken with neverending tryptophan-induced sleep. I guess what I'll say first off is that I'm not really a huge fan of so-called "flash fiction" or "short shorts"—I'm more of a fan of Tolstoy and DFW and, these days, *2666*. I like elaboration, theme and variation, associative opportunities, immersion in another world. Short pieces often feel like the beginning of a conventionally sized story, or a paragraph of one—unless it's a Russell Edson "poem," which feel self-contained, more like a joke. Maybe that's the way to think about short-short fiction, as a joke that's not funny but nevertheless moves you by the time the punch-line hits. With what you sent, the punch-line is the bit at the end about the King searching for the old accordion songs that don't exist—there's a soft "poignancy" thing going on related to longing for those songs. One issue I have with this is the line in the middle that begins, "They created myths about the accordion player," or more exactly, the word "the" before "accordion player," which makes the reader re-read to see if anything's been missed, i.e., which accordion player?! Also, I envisioned Elvis at first — the Kool-Aid also set me off in that direction. But then by the end, post-talk of peasants, it's more like a Hans Christian Anderson fable. And then in terms of syntax, something I really have some trouble with is the "meaningful word" at the end of a sentence set off by a comma, e.g., "undiscovered." That's all personal sensibility stuff, but also the reason for this response instead of another sort of response. Anyway — thanks for sending this and good luck finding a home for it and send more whenever.

Hey — sorry for the slowish reply — I really like the comparison of smoking on NYC fire escapes and kissing a girl with braces. Awesome. Afterwards, it felt like it relies too much on forward propulsion, moving too fast to actually say much maybe, or maybe to really transmit clear images to a reader? It's all blurry because, I think, you might be writing a bit too closely to yourself instead of trying to reach someone else across the great divide? In that way, this seems more like a long-sentencey stream-of-diary entry than a "story" per se, which may be your intention, but then for a diary-type thing you also don't offer enough juicy personal revelations to engage the reader's voyeuristic capacities. Also, we East Coast folks who have lived in NYC really need NYC-related writing to make us see it in a new way, like that first line about the fire escapes and braces (more of that and I'd've been psyched to post this). Also, I'm not a huge fan of Jeff Buckley — I find that a certain sort of sad lady always plays "Hallelujah" as an (ineffective) aphrodisiac/après-sexiness serenade. Anyway — thanks for sending this and send more whenever.

Honestly, this reads like you were stoned and had some fun dashing something off and then sent it. Sober, on my end, it's frustrating to read. It's not funny. It's pretty much juvenile. It's absurdist for the sake of, well, nothing. It's not controlled. It's nothing, really. These are only things I thought while reading, of course — other sites might think differently. But I bet you can do way better. Raise your game, Sir.

Our submission guidelines specifically say not to send anything involving dentists, or by extension, dentistry, even if it's historical dentistry.

Thanks for sending this. It reads clearly and cleanly and crispy (and all the other above-board C words that are components of the word CLARITY). Which is real good. But I guess the problem for me is that it makes me want to shout WHITE GIRL IN AFRICA! WHITE GIRL IN AFRICA! over and over until the words lose meaning and the scene on the bus transforms into something that might interest a reader beyond the literal evocation of the initially intoned WHITE GIRL IN AFRICA. Lots of people submit "stories" (scenes, really) that could be called My (Sort of) Interesting Experience in an Exotic Land. I've traveled some and have had some blatantly interesting experiences and some really subtle ones, too (somewhere on Eyeshot you can find a 100-page travelogue I posted about solo travel through Central America when I was 23), but I think it's important to maybe use the sketch or scene or sensation for some larger narrative or character or thematic purpose? Anyway, also, re: Eyeshot's hopes and dreams: I'm really mostly looking to post pieces that are sort of benevolently effed up (as the kids say) that are funny and dense and unpredictable and maybe begin exactly as your story starts but end up underground, feeding blood oranges and mythologically loaded pomegranates to a subterranean orangutan porn star. Something like that.

Thanks for sending this but I don't really think I'm going to post it. I hope that's ok with you. You seem like a good human being from what I can tell from your story. Sorry for not going into much detail re: the rationale re: this rejection. I am a bad human being. Forgive me.

To the writer,

No thanks.

Regards,

The editor.

This dies when you start talking about smooth skin. You're sort of setting something up but then you just drop it and start talking about chest hair. Tom Selleck = not funny.

Thanks for sending this to our "magazine." (Why would you call a site a magazine? Makes me question the depth of your "love.") Regardless, thanks again for sending this, but its meta-ness didn't really do anything except irritatingly stall a story that honestly seemed like an exercise in metafiction my undergrads might've done when I taught such things? Thanks again for sending it and good luck with this and other submissions elsewhere — and I hope you continue enjoying the Eyeshot magazine.

First, right away, the simile "could smile like mountains" threw me off — it's overblown and makes no sense, really. What's it seem to mean? A big choppy smile with ever-receding snowcaps? It's actually a sort of hideous, cartoonish image. A reader is just trying to see something clearly but you're trying too hard to provide something to see that you're getting in the way of a reader seeing "Erin's" existence. You have an admirable ambitious instinct but it gets in the way of simple/clear communication/creation of an intelligible image at this point?

Naw, dawg, but like yo how'm I gonna show this to my mama? Look, mama, look at what I've posted about Chris Garvey's pennis! It's... Wha, Mah? I'm sorry, Mah... Yes, ma'am. I should really grow up, I know... I will do my best to post more mature works about motes of dust in afternoon light.

Thanks for sending something again after so many years reading and submitting to the site. In exchange I'll try to do my best to answer your grad school questions. The whole process of reading applications to grad school is similar to the process of reading submissions for a publication—there's a ton of paper filled with imagined worlds, all evoked with varying success, all demonstrating varying degrees of mastery of English. At Iowa, I spent every day of the month of January 2006 reading at least 30 pages in about ten applications — I did not read every word. In fact, for a lot of applications, same as with submissions, I scanned the literary DNA of the first few pages and figured out more or less immediately if things had a chance. What did I look for? Authority, audacity, execution, and oomph. Those are the terms that revealed themselves after that grueling January solely reading 8.5 x 11s. They're interconnected, I think. Lord knows. Authority involves execution — the sense of storytelling control, a sense that "an intelligence pulses through the page" (what Frank Conroy apparently looked for in applications), and it requires basic grammar, word choice, storytelling dynamics execution (creation of scenes, characters, dialogue), inventiveness, facility, swerve. Authority also involves a sort of seriousness, a heft, even if the story is "funny"— think DFW or George Saunders, they use humor to get at fundamental human dealios. Audacity has more to do with, I think, the way a story might move, sudden switches of gear, or word choice. The Panda Suit itself is a good example of this, but it'd be WAY MORE AUDACIOUS if the narrator were an actual panda working at a grocery store, lusting after an actual giraffe with her human mom, right? Oomph is just an odd-looking substitute for narrative drive—VERY NECESSARY for an MFA application or a submission is to kick living shit out of the first page or two, to get the ball rolling, to tell a story, to give a character/narrator something s/he wants, a desire, or place an obstacle in front of them, a coming of night to rage against etc—otherwise, if the story just sort of opens up and floats along, the reader who's been reading every day all day through one of the darkest months of the year, isn't gonna love the story. Make sure your stories "tell a story"—start them on page three, if necessary. Drop a reader right in the bucket. No establishing shots necessary. OK—now the big question—why did every fucking MFA program pass on what you sent?! Note: they didn't reject you as a human being. They looked at your thing and compared it to others they received and chose others. It's possible that your thing was the 31st best but, like Iowa, they only accepted 30, assuming five wouldn't come and they'd field a class of 25 out of the 1000+ applicants each year. Holy hell, right? That's an optimistic way of thinking about it. Here are my totally subjective reasons, which you can take or leave: The title is intriguing, which is good. The first line is odd, fantastical maybe? A kingdom in a supermarket? Hmm. OK. Good. The first very red flag rises with the hyperalliteration involving F-words. (Fuck, dude.) Found, feeling up, frozen, flounder, fish—at that point all I'm doing is thinking "alliteration" and I'm not thinking it's a good thing at all. I'm not seeing beyond the language! Compare with Nabokov, Gass, Pynchon, everyone but Dean Koontz — stay away from alliteration unless it really elicits a laugh or helps propel a sentence through its rhythms, and don't start with it! After the F-barrage, I notice a minor B-barrage (bakery, burnt, battered), then a D-duo (department, department). Now I'm against you as a reader — I started neutral, leaning toward a natural disinclination due to the nature of my month-long plight. But now, midway through the all-important first glance (love at first sight? aversion?), you take us on a tour of the grocery store: I know what produce is, I don't need examples (lemons, lines — more alliteration!) A little lower down on page 2, there's the line: "On the evening in question" and I thought "huh?" There was no mention of an evening thus far. Later, the story is about the Giraffe, the clever (potentially cloying) thing about the panda suit, the party, some meatheads, and it ends with memories of playing music and feeling free. That's not really the "arc" of a successful story. Or, well, I don't really believe in such things — I believe a story can do anything, go anywhere, have a shape other than a gleaming porpoise curve momentarily outta water (see Stuart Dybek's story, "Paper Lanterns") that is, as long the language is enticing and controlled and pungent and ughfully awesome (i.e., every sentence reveals authority, execution, audacity, oomph). If not, if the language is not gonna win the day, we need some drama, seriously vivid characters who walk around and talk and DO something more than court each other or wear panda suits to parties, right? The language of what you sent is generally adequate for telling a story, but it doesn't really differentiate you from a lot of writers? I think you might benefit from putting more pressure on your language, really honing it, cutting as much as possible from a phrase till you can bounce a dime off it, vary length and syntax, compare side by side a page of your prose with a page of your favorite writer's prose. The language in this is fine, serviceable, but, per Salinger's phrase, it doesn't seem like "all your stars are out." Really go for it. Write by hand while highly caffeinated, scribble, do whatever it takes so you bust through the scrim of adequacy I sense in these pages —don't worry about making it new or screwing with language, just SEE as well as you can and transcribe what you imagine as fast as you can and then type it all up and deal with the mess in Word until it's comprehensible but still alive? I'm saying that what I've read seems hesitant instead of confident. I also think that this could be solved if the narrator were an actual panda — think of the unique VOICE, think of the potential for old-fashioned hilarity. And of course all the time the reader would be seeing around the narrator, knowing that he's not a panda. Part of the problem I had with these pages, also, is that, other than the panda suit, it's about a slacker guy who goes to a party in search of a girl. Maybe best to avoid that sort of story and that sort of character? I definitely wrote some similar stories involving sad young men with their quirks and developing sense of self lusting after lovely young ladies, but it's best to maybe only use that boy-girl story as a spine to get at larger things, like say the end of the world, or the revolutionary situation in Sri Lanka? I think for the future, for applying to MFA programs, you're way better off sending three or so stories — if you send an excerpt, clearly label it as a novel excerpt so the pressure is off a little, though more pressure will be on the sentences themselves. Mostly, keep in mind that tired snarky grad students are reading these things and they want someone to grab them with controlled, engaging, interesting, readable language that tells a moving story involving actual human beings, even if they're pandas, existing in a deeply imagined world. If you do that, everything else is CAKE. Sorry if I can't be all that positive about what you sent — I'd like to be, and I'm sure I could go through and find example of goodness throughout (I read a printout in a cafe on my lunch break and my pen died so I couldn't make notes and therefore am more general here than I'd like to be). Anyway, thanks and definitely let me know if you have specific questions about MFA programs or what I wrote above or what I didn't write. And thanks for reading Eyeshot since the innocent days of yore. It's really gotten sort of ugly and puffier lately — I try to stay offline as much as I can...

Thanks for sending something but it's really just not the sort of thing I'm looking to post. I'm really more interested in psychopathic overindulgence that's nevertheless innocent and doe-eyed and charming and like totally LOL.

So I guess I like want to like thank you for like sending this submission. "Cracking witticisms" felt like it was like a little off phrase-wise. Otherwise I guess what I mean to say is that, other than the conversational voice that I'm like sort of dubious about unless it's done by DFW, I guess I was sort of like maybe thinking this is like not quite right for this site I sort of like edit? And so but then like I was maybe thinking that you might not respond to this totally quick response from me with a "fuck yeah" but instead maybe something else more like FU or worse, and so I like decided that maybe the best way to like ameliorate shit right away and in like advance was to like maybe let you know that like whatever I think about this submission's boundness for the site I like edit, I nevertheless totally bet you're the total shit and I wish you well now and well beyond T-give, the burliest of holidays.

First, I guess that despite this being a little denser formally, content-wise it's not really in the same area code — or time zone, really — in terms of what I tend to post. Formally, there were two hurdles I couldn't jump in the first part: one was the repetition of "She felt" in two early sentences. Usually I'm against the old "show don't tell" thing because people tend to say "show don't tell" when they mean "dramatize action — don't summarize it," and that's something I wholly disagree with and can cite a billion canonical precedents for support — but I do agree with "show don't tell" when it's used as a suggestion about relaying a character's emotions. Maybe it's better not to say, for example, that a character is impatient—instead have her almost curse out a total stranger taking too much time in a crosswalk. The second thing I had trouble with is that you have way too many compound adjectives — each one felt like a cactus that kept snagging my attention as I ran down the screen in search of water (maybe each time you use a hyphen like in mocha-colored try to think up a better adjective or a different way of describing her brown hair). But thanks again for sending this and good luck and all. I guess I think overall that Eyeshot might not be the best spot for the stuff you've already written but might be a home for new stuff one day, maybe, assuming you write new stuff. Anyway, thanks and sorry and good luck.

Maybe because this one sort of just lobs the exclusive Country Club stereotype in the air, expecting it to do more than momentarily float before obeying the law of gravity, this one won't work for Eyeshot. Jokes re: rich folks and Botox aren't for us. Jokes re: mischievous gophers at Country Clubs are way more on target (i.e., a piece composed solely of "Caddyshack" references). Also, Thanksgiving was last week. Also, the third- and fourth-to-last paragraphs seemed a bit too meaty to get through.

I like the honest-seeming spirit of it. It's melodramatic and simple, with the language occasionally straining to create images — a believable impression of a lightly afflicted sixteen year old. I wrote similar stories when I started writing: a story about a disturbed young man (DYM) whose reflection wasn't there in the mirror (cleverly entitled "The Empty Mirror"), and a little later a story about a DYM walking from the outskirts of a city to its center to deliver a letter, all the while imaging all sorts of alternate letters he was sending and describing everything (EVERYTHING) he saw in great metaphorically significant and vaguely sad detail. After a while I tried to lose the DYM and write more about myself as I really was, with a sense of humor and a little more bounce to my step, or about other people and the actual world they lived in. I tried to tell stories, too. Actual stories — not abstract textual vessels loaded with loaded details. Not saying that what you sent isn't a story, just that for Eyeshot at least, I'm not necessarily interested in posting DYM stories, unless DYM can fly or transforms midway into a bowl of pasta on which his pop's about to sprinkle grated cheese.

Is this a plagiarized excerpt from a James Bond book I never read? It's really not right for the site, regardless. Sorry. But thanks for sending it.

I guess the problem I have, or the difficulty, the CHALLENGE here, for me, for you, is that I like language that's maybe a little less pungent, a little less in service of itself than a story (no matter how screwed/strange), YET I also like the language to look lovely and move quickly and unpredictably. I mainly like language that relays intelligible (clear) meaning and sensory information, doing so with pace and unpredictable movement. What you sent is very attentive, but it feels to me too much like pinned butterflies — the sentence with the semi-colon at the end, followed by a word, particularly. It's a sense that you're really paying attention to writing "beautiful" language but the meaning is too elusive, the train of thought too trackless for me? And that's why I pass despite admiring the attentiveness of the language—it's ultimately just one reader over on this end and thousands of others out there who will surely respond more favorably, although again I'm not responding unfavorably, just that I don't think what you've sent is exactly the sort of thing I've tended to post on Eyeshot over the last 9.5 years.

I liked the bookstore setting and the mystery about the book at first (why would guy flip it off? Why's everyone buying it?) and then I liked the repetitions, but then it sort of fell apart, got metafictional about metafiction, and ended with anguish and anger that seemed to come from nowhere (it wasn't earned as creative writing dips might say, in an italicized, vaguely British way). So I guess I'll thank you again and say I was right there with you for about 60% of it and then felt the carpet slide out from under me.

I managed to read this one from beginning to end (a compliment!) and I should say that it's not every day that I receive readable submissions involving Goth robot vampire communist assassin sluts. I sort of like how ridiculous it is but then again it's ridiculous in a way that maybe felt a bit too cartoonishly gumshoe to me? How else could it feel though? Not sure. Not sure about the erotic stuff either. I don't think I'll post it, ultimately, but I'll wish you luck and totally look forward to what you send next.

I guess what I should say is that this story, while readable and not annoying, isn't what I'm looking to post on Eyeshot right now. If I were to post it, I'd be flooded with similar stories by dudes about going to see bands. My life would not improve. I would not smile more. I would not post any of these stories, either. Instead, I want to post stories that make me laugh or at least smile, and that would make others momentarily happy to have come to Eyeshot and read some strange, funny, well-done story that might not find a home at respected journals and sites. Plus, the more strange and funny stories I post, the more of those stories people will send, and my life will improve through the winter (as Gil Scott Heron once sang, it's winter in America).

I'd say it's a primo example of something that's perfectly amusing yet not necessarily "funny." The title makes it seem like it was probably a McSweeneys.net submission at one point, and the execution is perfectly clear and all, but I didn't hear myself laugh. I did like the stuff about Buddha at the end, though. But I thank you for sending this and I wish you well with this bit of writing and other stories and stuff related to the first tenet of Buddhism (all life = suffering). Anyway, please have a sufferingless new year and send again whenever.

I really like the cougar urine early on and would like to read a story about how someone figured out that cougar urine works wonders in terms of turning away varmits from one's garden. Think about that — it's crazy — how do you figure something like that out? An excellent idea for a story: part serious historical research, part insane character, part cougar. Write it and I'll read it posthaste. Otherwise, "rots rats guts from the inside out" seemed like a phrase that you enjoyed writing too much for a reader not to stop and think that the writer enjoyed writing it a lot. "Spelunked" should be avoided in terms of rooting through garbage, though it's fine for eating chocolate chunk ice cream or rooting around in one's mouth with one's member? "Princess Leah" ain't right — it's Leia. But otherwise, the story just didn't have the right sort of vibe for what I'd like to vibrate Eyeshot's readers with. Sorry! But thanks and please send a story about the provenance of cougar urine.

Thanks for sending something — I assume you've seen the Herzog documentary about Antarctica? If not, you're in for a treat. The relevant bit can be seen if you google "Herzog Antarctica penguins youtube" and I almost sorta maybe kinda considered accepting this because of its relation to the Herzog doc (and to one of my favorite bits in it), but I think generally, for Eyeshot, it was maybe a little long, definitely too dialoguey, too straight, and a little too something or other I can't quite articulate right now because my brain is a little fogged after dinner and a long day of professional office-based editorial work? You understand, right? I hope you do! I'm sayin' I understand the compulsion to head to the mountains, but maybe for Eyeshot's purposes the opening might clarify that Sam and Leonard aren't human-type people right away — if this occurred in a film or on stage, we'd see two penguin-type people right away, but instead there's that initial confusion, which actually might have accounted for my aforementioned brain fog more than postprandial mental letdown? I mean, sure, the freakin title mentions a damn penguin, but right away I was looking at Sam and Leonard, undescribed white American dudes (~23-32 years old), not formally attired Arctic fowl, and so maybe I didn't quite trust things or didn't dig in as much as I would've if I'd been fully oriented from the get go? Black and white words, black and white birds. There's something to mess with there. Generally, Herzog association or not, it's a cute little existential parable with suggestions of deeper familial sadness, but again for Eyeshot I prefer stories like this after they've been held by the ankles and had their carefully coiffed hair flushed to a fine swirl in the toilet, and there's that unnecessary opening disorientation. Anyway, thanks again for sending and send again whenever.

REJECTION LETTERS FROM THE EYESHOT OUTBOX

PLEASE CONSULT OUR GUIDELINES! WE COULD NOT BE MORE EMPHATIC REGARDING EYESHOT-BRAND ANTIPATHY REGARDING STORIES REGARDING THE PROFESSION OF DENTISTRY! NEVER AGAIN DENTISTS! NO DENTISTS! NO!

Okay. I read your "Mike" story again, closely and slowly, knowing what you told me about its origin, while sipping chicken soup on my birthday. I am an old man now. And maybe because in the northeast we have this thing called "wintertime" that makes one dark and depressive and sometimes slow to coddle whimsy, especially as one gets older and colder and becomes more aware of what some might think is a super-sad state of the world, the corruption and inequalities and generally accepted idiocies et cetera, maybe because of all this I am a bit resistant to the idea of a breakfast burglar? Oddly, right now in Philly there's a foot fetishist who late at night holds up women and massages and kisses their feet. But I guess what I like about this story is the third section, after the introductory disorientation with Martha and the clarifying quote about the narrator's history, when it gets more into the father/son dynamics, but it doesn't really go too far into it, and sadly relies on semi-typical queer stuff. It seems to this reader at least that you had a bright idea based on something you'd heard, something you know about but the reader does not, but then when you relate that information I don't feel the enthusiasm you must have had at first for the idea, I'm not infected with it at least, in part because the story seems fragmented, constructed in four parts instead of an integrated whole? Or maybe it didn't seem to engage me enough from the beginning, or maybe I'm a little more resistant to whimsicality now more than ten years ago, or maybe the serious elements I'm engaged by in the story seemed dragged down by the whimsicality and the weirdness of the idea of a breakfast burglar? Does that make sense? I'd like to love this but you are not this piece of writing, and if you're to have any love for me you've got to respect that I am not going to be anything other than 100% earnest about my response. I'd be an asshole in the long run, otherwise, on this my special day. I have three or four stories I've worked 4000 hours on, stories seven times longer than what you sent, stories I've submitted everywhere and have been sort of semi-close (or at least apparently closely read) at some of the best places and other places too but no one ultimately accepts them and they should totally freakin' be published, of course (!), but finally it comes down to the response of one or two people — and there's nothing a writer can do about it but work and keep sending out the things you love and feel confident about no matter the response by fuckers like me! So. Sorry, again, but to say anything other than what's above would be totally immoral.

Thanks for sending something — the first paragraph seems intentionally and atrociously overwritten—a gorgeous example of intentionally and atrociously overwritten prose. It's so overburdened with modifiers that there's no way it can't be intentional, a sort of joke, and as such assuming it's a joke I didn't quite laugh but ocularly macheted my way through to what came after, which seemed to me like a cartoonish presentation of a blocked cartoon of a sad ego-inflated writer in a Hawaiian print shirt, before it slipped into pages of dialogue I honestly skimmed because Eyeshot specifically doesn't really champion dialogue-heavy stories. The world of writing online is full of talk but we've always been about swervy dense blocks of sentences. If we do post something talky it's most likely exaggeratedly off or does something unexpected or is flat-out funny. That's just the way it is. Sorry. But thanks again for sending this and good luck with it and everything else, including your upcoming fantasy football draft, which I expect will go very very well.

Signed,
Eyeshot's Chinch-Bug in Chief

Thanks for sending something to Eyeshot. We appreciate getting old-fashioned e-mail these days. It reminds me of old-fashioned postal mail, what once were called letters. It's especially nice when these e-mails come equipped with little blips from the brains of recent Stanford grads, from intelligent human life forms existing 3000 miles away, although of course whenever we want we all exist in the same place these days, everywhere and nowhere online. First up, re: the submission, there's a typo in the first paragraph: "touched gently on the the back of her neck." It shouldn't really make a difference, it's just a typo, but it derails an editor's entry and for a split second makes editor wonder about the degree of effort expended on the submitted piece, that is, it begs the question how closely should the editor read the submission if typos exist, but of course since the editor is a writer himself he knows that such typos occur when one makes a last second change and doesn't see it until some freakin editor 3000 miles away responds and goes on and on about it, and then even self-indulgently does so in an annoying, self-critical, meta way that's totally uncalled for, even from a pissant so-called literary website. But the typo is meaningless — fix it and forget about it! What matters more with this is the subject matter and the tone? Seems like you totally miss out on using the heft of the dying newborn to your advantage? Your tone is whimsical and the events that occur are whimsical, like the imminent death of the newborn is just a jumping off point for whimsy? I like the idea of everyone ganging together to give the doomed neonate a world tour of everything he's gonna miss out on but I think I might have been more interested in this if it were more about mothereffin baby death, if the specter of it hung over

REJECTION LETTERS FROM THE EYESHOT OUTBOX

everything, if the tone were darker and foreboding and the mother and the nurses and everyone were doing their best to entertain the doomed kid while the mother sat there drugged, the whole thing really freakin sad... maybe more from the drugged perception of a mother handed down the death sentence, presented more seriously, with language less willing to show that the writer's paying lots of attention to word choice and syntax — just trying to mainline the serious heft of imminent baby death mixed with the skewed perception of the world tour of life seen through the disturbed mother's drugged eyes? I'm finally articulating this better, I think. These are just the thoughts of a writer/reader 3000 miles away from you, miraculously fresh-headed after a Friday night of moderate intake of fancy beer, jacked now on coffee, of course, but also you had me interested at first since I think every day about the baby in my wife's belly (she's about five months along) coming out skewed or behorned or bewinged or worse — strangulated, stillborn, turned to stone — and my wife definitely spends most of her time sleeping on her side. Thus. Therefore. Maybe think about re-focusing the POV a bit more on the heft of infant baby death and filtering what's currently straight-up whimsy so it's more a product of distressed mama's drugged perception? This would require a total re-write in tone and perspective but it might be worth it. Just watched a pretty good documentary called "The Business of Being Born," produced by Ricki Lake, that might provide some ideas for lampooning here. And if all else fails there's always that Monty Python birthing bit in *The Meaning of Life*. Anyway, good luck with it and thanks again and please excuse excessive rejectionary word count. Coffee is really strong this morning...

Thanks for submitting. Can I ask some questions? How did you find Eyeshot? Who are your favorite authors and did they influence the story you sent? What does it mean that you've "been edited"? Have you written more than four stories and the novel? Is the story "enclosed" or "attached"? It's attached, right? It would be enclosed if it were in an envelope? Why are you looking for an agent? Why do you want to get your "foot in the door of the literary world"? What does that mean anyway? I ask these questions not only because the Eyeshot Editor has a history of responding to submissions thusly but also because I'm interested in your responses. It's interesting to me to see how people go about trying to write and publish, to see where their heads are in terms of hopes, expectations re: the so-called "lit world," but also idealism re: art.

There are no real rules. But there are unreal rules related to taste, to intuition, to textually triggering some corner of the pineal gland, which when set off by something semi-inexplicable in a succession of words, engages this reader at least, lets one's third eye see something not there — we're talking neurologic magic, man. Imagination induction. That's the only rule. Make someone see something that's not there via a succession of engaging words. Also, if possible, vaguely amaze and if possible make laugh. Do that and you can make whatever rules you want.

I totally suck for passing on this, so please send again whenever, and keep at it, never give up the good fight, and read, read, read. Sorry, and thanks, and may you live a life of well-received, restless production and consistent good health. Take care. Goodnight. Thanks and sorry and good luck!

EYESHOT'S UNNECESSARILY LONG-WINDED SUBMISSION GUIDELINES

Eyeshot has been internationally accessible since 1999. Fiction, photographs, rants, reviews, links, essays, and other unclassifiables are accepted and declined. We pay in dissemination and validation, however meager.

Eyeshot prefers electronic (i.e., e-mailed) submissions. We do not use Submishmasochism or whatever it's called these days. Although we admire the ease of these interfaces, for Eyeshot's purposes, we prefer to work the nostalgia tip and make things seem a little old-fashioned—thus, for now, send submissions to submit at eyeshot.net.

(Note: if you have no idea what Eyeshot usually posts and are just sending scattershot submissions to sites listed on the devil's own Duotrope, please send submissions to pissoff@dickweed.org.)

Here are some further ideas: Please include boatloads of biographical information and links to every possible previous publication and the name of every professor you ever heard speak or slept with at your prestigious NYC MFA program you'll soon graduate from +$80K in debt, and—very important!—make sure to mention how many times you've been nominated for a Pushcart Prize. We would also like to see links to most if not all of your social media accounts, especially Goodreads, Twitter, Uganda, Tumblr, Whatnot, and Facebook. If you would like to start a Kickstarter fundraiser thing to raise money for a bribe to grease our editorial palms, please do so well in advance of your submission. (Note: we can be bribed pretty easily these days but when it comes to bills we prefer larger more than smaller.)

SPECIFIC RECOMMENDATIONS & RESTRICTIONS

Once there was a time when asked about submission guidelines we consulted the many sages and they all replied, "Cows never roam from pastures with no fences." We can't deny the wisdom of the sages. And so we figured there shan't be submission guidelines. EXCEPT, to recognize that some people might want to know what we tend to post without bothering to browse the archive, we are now happy to offer somewhat explicit recommendations:

DO NOT SEND POETRY unless 1) it's disguised as prose, 2) it's totally nasty and perverted, or 3) you're an Egyptian.

PLEASE TRY NOT TO SEND if your e-mail address includes the words writer, write, poet, or anything similar. If you are under 17 years of age, it's OK. But otherwise, please do not submit.

PLEASE TRY NOT TO SEND whimsical pieces loaded with dialogue and lots of lame pop-cultural references (we prefer mythological, literary, art-historical, and/or misanthropomorphophagical allusions).

PLEASE TRY NOT TO SEND something about an emotionally cathartic moment from your childhood (unless it involves dead clowns).

PLEASE TRY NOT TO SEND some small, relatively unimaginative, essayistic piece about deli meats or chapstick or dentists.

PLEASE TRY NOT TO SEND anything that anyone would ever describe as "punk rock."

PLEASE TRY NOT TO SEND anything if your favorite author is Bukowski. Nothing against the man, but if he's your favorite author, please send your submission elsewhere. Again, we have no real problem with Bukowski's writing whatsoever, but if you're all about him, that is, if you write like him way more than you write like yourself, please realize you're invited to 1) pray for a big ol' rainstorm of sweet, sweet whisky, and 2) insert and piston your skinny ashen thingy (assuming you're a boy) into and out of the hole in the center of your collector's edition DVD of "Barfly."

PLEASE TRY NOT TO SEND anything that you would call "flash fiction." Short pieces are fine to send, but not if you refer to them as "flash fiction." We seem to have a problem with the term.

PLEASE REALIZE you can send any of the above but we won't accept them unless they're really funny and/or wonderful. We tend to like things that are denser (not so quick to include space breaks between sentences), that are somewhat elusive and inventive and overblown languagewise and not-so-sane aesthetically. OK? That's a hint intended to save us all time. But then again, we're always open to reading anything you want to send. It may seem like there are now some fences, but they're imaginary fences. If you don't want them to be there, that's fine— think of them as suggested fences.

PLEASE REALIZE that these days we will only have fun with our rejection letters if you send your submission via the post in an envelope loaded with cold hard cash. Or bribe us first via PayPal. The more money you send the more performatively and possibly helpfully we'll reject the little that we read. Please don't think that including a dollar will get you much in terms of rejection, or that sending $20 will entice us to accept the story. Basically, if you're feeling masochistic and need some creative rejection in your life, you can buy our services. Ten volumes of collected rejection letters accessible on the site may prove an invaluable resource for prospective submitters interested in discerning our editorial tendencies and taste.

PLEASE REALIZE we're no longer encouraging visitors to send stuff that's plagiarized or transcripts of instant messages, although we did in the past (before folks started using gchats in their fiction, FYI).

If you would like to send physical objects (manuscripts, $$$, gifts, small cat toys, or books/music), our mailing address is: Eyeshot, PO Box 18009, Phila, PA 19147